Stable of Studs

Misadventures in Dating and Relationships

Mary Walsh

Discover other books by Mary Walsh

The Curse of Jean Lafitte
Knights of the Corporate Round Table
American Posse
Memories of 9/11
Plenty of Fish in the Ocean State
Once Upon a Time in Chicago
His Second Chance
Dragon Slayer
Catch a Break
Life Lessons for my Kids
Fine Spirits Served Here
Where or When
Wounded but not Dead
You Deserve Better

Copyright
Published by Mary Walsh
©2017 Mary Walsh

All rights reserved
marywalshwrites.com

Stable of Studs

Chapter 1

Single Again

The day after a break-up, I lamented to my friend Chris about how this last guy blindsided me. I replayed the break-up in my mind repeatedly, trying to figure out what I did wrong.

"I liked that guy too, so it was unexpected. I guess that's what I get for liking someone," I moaned.

"Don't beat yourself up," Chris consoled me. "You didn't discover this guy's poor judgment until yesterday. Better to learn that sooner rather than later. I'm guessing he has a lot of hidden issues that cloud his judgment."

"I think he was afraid of being tied down and had commitment issues," I replied. Pausing, I looked back on some of the conversations I'd had with this last one. "Yes. A lot of commitment issues. I'm sure of it."

"He probably had one or more cats." We both laughed. "Wish I could make you feel better," Chris replied.

"Just tell me that it wasn't me," I pleaded.

Chris shook his head. "I can't lie to you, love. Seems like you have picked some real head cases. That's something you should work on...picking non-head cases. You gotta hone those skills. Do some reflection and figure out why you continue to choose these types of guys."

Frustrated because my feelings were hurt, but wanting to hear what I could do better, I cried out, "How? By going out with a bunch of people? And what? Seeing who or what is out there?"

"Exactly. More data can help if you're a good observer." With a degree in math and methodical, Chris looked at this like a data analyst.

I scoffed. "Can't I observe from behind a glass window?"

"This is your love life," Chris explained. "You are the case study and the scientist. You cannot leave the work to anyone else. Unfortunately, what you are perceiving depends on you being part of the equation."

He had a point. Chris and I had been great friends for 25 years and he understood me inside and out. He didn't have to sugarcoat and I didn't get offended when he called me out on the various "head cases" I had chosen. But he also reaffirmed that I grasped what felt right, what didn't, what I valued most in life, and what I didn't value much. I had a plan for what I wanted for myself and my kids.

Throughout it all, Chris also told me that he envied my perseverance. He pointed out that lots of people gave up on their dreams and settled, but my refusal to compromise showed how strong I was.

Nervous to get back out and date again so quickly after being hurt, but I couldn't hide behind a glass window and watch, either. I had so many fears: Scared of getting hurt again. Scared of hurting someone else. Scared of the crazies lingering in the figurative shadows. Scared that I would be alone. Scared that I wouldn't find the right guy for me. Scared to make myself vulnerable. Scared of the nonsense of dating.

No one would be climbing a tower wall to find their Rapunzel. Besides, I didn't want to be rescued. I wanted to be found. And yes, sometimes the best relationships are the ones we aren't looking for, but I still had to be proactive. Sitting on my couch 24/7 wouldn't help me meet anyone.

I believe in love. Really, I do. Being with someone is a nice feeling. I'm not afraid to be alone, but I'm also not a hermit. I would like to spend my life with someone.

Being married for 13 volatile years didn't turn me off from the institution. I still believe that good people exist and I have learned how to spot a douchebag. As a result, I do have hope that I'll meet someone.

Some days I want to give up or can't be bothered. But I understand I can't do that if I want to find someone.

While I'm waiting, I'll share my love life experiences with you and document what I have learned along the way. I will tell you right now that I might get my heart broken. I might break someone's heart. I might meet someone great who still feels off (you know what I'm saying). I'll tell you about my dates and my text exchanges and my friends' opinions. If you're willing to follow me on my journey, you'll read that I'm willing to put it all out there.

I am looking forward to this adventure. In the process, I also hope that other women (and possibly men) can learn from my encounters and realize they are awesomely confident, self-aware, and secure.

I considered blogging everything out, but honestly, I don't want to be a slave to a website. Nor do I want any of my followers to leave nasty comments about me or any of the men I encounter. My former romantic partners don't need to learn about my journey and I'd like to keep their identities hidden as much as possible.

I've done my homework and read Steve Harvey's *Act Like a Lady, Think Like a Man* and Greg Behrendt *He's Just Not That Into You*. I get that I should move on if a man doesn't meet my needs. I also shouldn't chase anyone, as I have learned that the man likes the chase.

I have acquired the skill of not being, what Steve Harvey calls, a "chirp-chirp girl." A "chirp-chirp girl" is a girl who is going on a date and the guy chirps his car door open with his remote and she robotically gets into his car. No! No! No! She needs to make him open that car door. On most occasions, ladies deserve that gesture.

If I ever encounter a man who doesn't automatically open the car door for me, then I'll remain at the curb and wait until he does. Sure, I might look like an idiot standing by myself, but I'll make a point. That man will either grasp that he should open the car door for me and appreciate that I am a lady or he'll be the one left at the curb because I won't put up with it again.

While we are on that topic, he needs to walk with me and not 10 steps ahead. Just because I might be eight inches shorter than a man does not automatically mean that I can keep up with his leg span. He needs to walk slower with me, not the other way around.

I've come up with a few basic rules of etiquette for first dates. You should already grasp good table manners, don't drink excessively, and be conscious of what you order. (Skip the onions, poppy seeds, and quinoa.) Maybe these few simple tips will help secure a second date?

Don't assume that you are entitled to the meal. When a man pays for dinner, thank him for the meal. That's the right thing to do. And, if the two of you go on later dates, don't hesitate to pay the bill sometimes. I'm sure he'll appreciate seeing that you don't expect him to pay for everything. Plus, he may like to be treated occasionally.

Have good manners on dates. Don't be rude, insulting, or judgmental. Don't ask about your date's salary or debt, or brag about your own. Don't curse or say things like "OMG" or "BFF." Be nice to the bartender, the waitress, and the taxi driver. A little kindness goes a long way.

Dress well. My friend Tom told me about this girl he met on a first date. When she showed up for their dinner in a t-shirt and yoga pants, he asked her if she came from yoga class. She gave him a confused look. He didn't ask her out again. The reason: she couldn't be bothered to even try to dress up for their date. Both parties need to put some effort into their appearances. On my first dates, I'll usually wear a skirt and a nice top or a cute dress. I'd like the guy to wear something decent as well. No shorts (unless we are doing something outside in the summer) and absolutely no sneakers or sweatshirts. If it's cold, he can wear a sweater. An ironed button-down shirt and nice shoes always work. Just sayin'.

Call if you will be more than five minutes late. No one likes the feeling of being stood up, especially on a first date. Be respectful of the other person's time. Everyone has a cell phone these days, so it is inexcusable not to call if you are running late – even if you are simply stuck in traffic. If you are more than 15 minutes late and don't call ahead, I wouldn't expect a second date with the person.

Don't talk about your ex, good or bad. If you say good things about your ex, your new date might think that you are still hung up on him. Don't say bad things about an ex either. You sound like a bitter person. If your date proactively asks you about your ex, stick to the 10 words or less version and try to be as diplomatic as possible.

Put your phone away – not on the table, but away. Put it in your pocket or your bag. Get it out of sight. The person in front of you should always be more important than any text message, phone call, or what's happening on Facebook. The only exception is an emergency phone call from your kid. If that happens, apologize profusely to your date and try to keep the phone call as short as possible. Or, if your date has not already turned off his phone or is making glances at it, make a game out of it. Both people put their phones in the middle of the table and whoever touches their phone first, pays for dinner. (Maybe that should be a game for a future date because the guy should always pay for the first date. Always.)

Don't tell a first date that you Googled them. Try not to Google them at all, but, if you can't resist, don't tell them that you've done so. You may come off as creepy, even though, ironically, everything we put online isn't private. If you discover something off about them online (like an assault charge), invent an excuse to cancel the date.

If the date goes badly and you have no intention of seeing the person again, don't indicate that you are open to a second date. Save him the after-date angst of "why isn't she calling me back?" He might thank you for it later. At the end of the date, simply shake his hand, thank him for dinner, say it was good to meet him, and leave it at that. Don't say anything like "Let's do this again sometime...", because he might think next Saturday is "sometime." Tell him that you don't want to date him again and say something like "I'm not the one for you." Give him that courtesy without disappearing.

Lastly, the age-old question of "to kiss or not to kiss?" I think it all depends on the chemistry of everyone involved and how well the date went. If you don't want to look too presumptuous, but still want the person to think that you are interested in him, a kiss on the cheek is almost always a good thing. But what if he leans in to kiss you and you aren't feeling the same? You can always say you have a rule that you don't kiss someone on the first date.

Lesson #1: Treat every date with respect. Always.

Chapter 2

The List

Have you heard of the TV show *Married at First Sight*? The title alone might scare off some people, but a panel of relationship experts matches couples together based on their personality traits and those people then don't meet until they convene at the altar. They skip the whole bad date phase and go straight to the partner chosen for them. Would I marry a total stranger? Absolutely not. But think about it... The show takes the emotions and angst out of meeting someone and matches couples based strictly on their compatibility. Maybe those experts are on to something?

Well, since most of us don't have the luxury of appearing on a television show to find our life partner, we have to use more traditional methods to identify a prospective mate. That process starts with "The List."

Many writers who claim they grasp the tricks to dating preach to make yourself a list of the qualities that you want in a partner. Great idea in concept, but usually no one gives out ideas to use. I have a few things in mind, but how long is this list supposed to be? I hate to be too picky. God knows if a man had a big list, I might not hit every single item on it. But I have to be realistic, right? I'll start with a few things and add to them as I learn more, so I may amend it in a later chapter. Here is my list so far:

1. He must be a non-smoker.

This is non-negotiable. I have never smoked and I hate the smell of cigarettes. Besides, I like having healthy lungs. An occasional cigar stokes the coolness factor, but I wouldn't want it to be a regular thing.

2. He must like kids and want to be around them.

I have two teenagers and I refuse to have a separate dating life and a separate mom life. I'll keep my kids out of the initial dates. But if a man tells me he can't get serious with a woman who has kids, no matter how much I like him, I'll have to move on. I won't waste my time on someone who refuses to meet my kids.

3. No drug use.

Again, non-negotiable. I have never been into the drug scene and don't care to start now. Nor will I babysit an addict.

4. He must have a job (and a car) and live by himself.

He needs to support himself. I am too old to deal with a slacker who permanently lives with roommates – or worse, his parents. Nightmares of all-night fraternity parties run through my head. Nor will I drive someone around or share my car.

5. He must have a handle on his money.

I have worked long and hard to have complete control of my finances and my partner needs to grasp his money outflow, not spending frivolously. I am not paying someone else's debts. Nor am I worrying about him coming home to a dark house because he didn't pay his electric bill. True story.

6. He needs to keep a clean house.

His home doesn't have to resemble a museum, nor does he have to vacuum every day. But I don't want to run from his house screaming if laundry is all over the floor, kitchen countertops have no vacancy, or week-old dishes sit in the sink collecting who knows what. I don't want to go into his house thinking to myself, "You'll be fine if you don't touch anything..."

7. No cheating.

This is a no-brainer and, for those who have even the smallest ounce of self-respect, it should be on everyone's list. Gray areas exist before two people are in an exclusive relationship, but I'll come back to that later. But if we are monogamous, no sexting, flirting, or touching another person in the wrong places.

I have standards, but I can also say that I hit every single one of those items if they are on a guy's list. I'd also want compatible personalities, a good sense of humor, and similar goals and values.

This seems like pretty basic stuff, right? I am aware that our hearts cloud our minds and we don't always follow our lists, but we should if we will ever be truly happy with someone. Our hearts sometimes stray and convince our heads that someone might be good for us when they are not. We must think pragmatically.

I don't care about tattoos, piercings, ethnicity, or body hair. Those items do not make the man. One of the nicest men I've ever met (the husband of an acquaintance) had longer hair than mine, a tattoo sleeve, and he often wore a skull cap. He had more character in his pinky than some other conservatively dressed men I have met.

If men can have a roster of women, why can't I have a stable of studs? Men shuffle women in and out of their lives without attachment or commitment. Why can't I date like a man to find the person that I want to be with for the rest of my life? I have heard this basic concept referred to as megadating. I don't intend to use guys at all, but I want to meet as many as possible to determine who the best candidate is for me. Like a job interview. I'll have fun with the ego boost and keep an open mind. I am not getting any younger, so I need to speed up the process of meeting the man for me. This seems like a good way to do it. I won't commit to someone until I deem that he is a good contender for me. I can't ever assume we are exclusive until we talk about it.

To narrow the pool even further, I want to stay away from dating any co-workers. My workplace doesn't have rules about dating, but I choose not to. I like to keep my private life separate from my professional life. Nor do I want to be headlining any intra-office gossip.

Plenty of nice men exist, but I don't want to settle for someone who doesn't make my heart jump at least a little. I am not willing to compromise what I want with what I get. I want to say, "See that awesome guy over there... Yeah, he's with me!" I want to be proud of the man that I am with.

If I have a relationship with someone for the sake of having the relationship and not because I am in love with the guy, it's a waste of my time (and his). If I can tell after a couple of months that I'll never truly be in love with the guy, I'll do the right thing and end it. I don't want to marry someone I can live with... I want to marry someone I can't live without.

Lesson #2: Create a list for yourself and figure out what kind of person you want.

Chapter 3

About Me

Now that you understand what I want, without being a total egomaniac, let me tell you more about me as a person. Where do I begin? Physical stuff is always a good start. Well, I'm 5'3" and petite. I have green eyes and light brown hair that reaches halfway down my back. Many men have told me that I am hot and that I have a nice body. Always good to hear, but I don't consider myself model material, nor do I have the desire to keep up that kind of appearance. For example, I think manicures are a waste of my money because I constantly do things with my hands. I like to wear girly dresses with heels, but I am also comfortable in jeans and a t-shirt.

I've always loved this vintage quote from actress Kathleen Turner: "There are some nights when I have power. I know I can put on something and walk in somewhere, and if there is a man who isn't looking at me, it's because he is gay." Every woman is beautiful and should have that kind of confidence.

I am in my mid-40s, but I look young for my age and often get carded (one time in front of my boss and co-workers... how humiliating). One day, while shopping for basketball socks with my son, I presented my credit card to the male clerk, who looked to be in his early 20s. He asked for my driver's license to confirm my identity. (Glad that clerks are doing this...)

He took a long look at my ID and said, "Girl, you look like you are 19 in this picture."

I pointed to my son and said, "That would be kind of hard when I have a teenage son."

The clerk then turned to my son and said, "Buddy, you have a hot mom."

My son rolled his eyes and walked away. He thought, "Dude, that's my *mom*!"

I like to be active and do things outside, but I am not a gym rat by any means. I don't have the time for it. On a hot day last summer, I found out how out of shape I was when I went to the pool and swam some laps. My heart jumped out of my chest, but I felt great and it was a good way to clear my head.

My wrist has been watch-less since college, but I almost always arrive on time and expect the same from others. I didn't get my first smartphone until November 2014 (I know... I know... get with the times...), but I didn't need it for work, nor did I want to post every moment of my life on Facebook or Instagram. I put up with the jabs until I realized the benefits of having one.

The two halves of my brain are constantly at odds with each other because I have a degree in Math, but I love painting and writing. Hopefully, they can do amazing things when they work together.

My garden is full of vegetables and I like to cook good food. What do I consider good food? Anything fresh, flavorful, and doesn't come out of a box. Besides, who wants those nasty preservatives in their body?

(Hmm, looks like I just wrote an online dating profile for myself. More on that later.)

I am constantly on the go with my teenagers' activities: soccer, basketball, cross country, musicals, field hockey, baseball, college tours, etc. I have 50/50 custody of them, alternating full weeks. My son and daughter have so much going on in their lives that it's nice for them to hang their hats at my place for a while before rushing off again. They probably don't like it when I tell them to put their phones away at the dinner table, but I want to teach them genuine social skills and how to interact with other people. I have been told many times that they are respectful kids and that I am a great mom. I try my best and hope that they appreciate everything that I am trying to teach them. (Even though my son might not agree with that when I tell him to pick up his mountain of shoes in the living room.)

Independent, I own my own home, cut my grass and shovel my snow, except when I make my son do it. I don't think that I am needy; I can take care of myself. If I am dating someone, I'd like to see them only a couple of times a week, because I don't want someone constantly in my face. Besides, I don't want to have to shave my legs every day!

Smart, insightful people make up my company of men and women. I am lucky to have great friends. My family lives up and down the East Coast, so my friends are my surrogate family. I was especially grateful when 20 of them came out to help me celebrate my 40th birthday. We help each other move, go out for dinner, work on house projects, share crazy stories about our kids and exes, and pick each other up when we get our hearts broken. Though lately, I'm primarily the one with the broken heart, since a lot of my friends are remarried or in long-term relationships. I couldn't ask for better friends. And fortunately, they don't mind me talking about them here.

In that group, I have a lot of male friends. Some of them have wives or girlfriends. Others don't. Some of them even have gaggles of kids. These guys are my brothers-in-arms when my two biological brothers aren't available. We share corny juvenile jokes ("How about that lawyer named Wayne Kerr?") and witty, bordering on stupid, observations that we find online.

When I asked one of my friends why he hadn't proposed to his long-term girlfriend and I wasn't satisfied with his answer, I mused, "Why buy the cow when I can get the milk for free? But then again, maybe she's thinking, why buy the pig when I can get the sausage for free?"

My male friends and I tell each other things that we might not tell our significant others. These male friends are my biggest fans and they're fiercely protective of me. If a guy hurts me or insults me, I have a posse he'll have to answer to. These male friends don't sugarcoat anything and they'll tell me to get my head out of my ass when I need to. That's something my female friends might not always do. In return, I ask these male friends hard questions and they won't judge me or get mad at me if I put them on the spot. I completely trust them and we have a mutual understanding that they won't gossip. Anyone that I might date cannot be jealous that I have male friends.

Whenever I need a pick-me-up, I reread an email that my almost-married friend Colin wrote to me after a guy decided I wasn't the right one for him. Colin's message said: "If his affection for you, his measurement of your worth, is not enough to give him the strength to overcome the obstacles... Do you even want him? It sounds like either weakness, cowardice, or deceit/boredom... neither of those things is a great foundation for more than a fling. I can see your value and, if I were in his position and taking his sentiment at face value... nothing would stop me. You are exceptional and I would say that any man that isn't willing to make an exceptional effort is likely not who you built him up to be in your mind. He's a big dumb idiot for tossing you aside. Wise men don't make mistakes like that." Thank you, Colin. I needed that.

Lesson #3: Determine who you are and what your best assets are.

Chapter 4

Misadventures of Online Dating

I finally took the online dating plunge in early 2014. I had broken up with The Professor (more on him later) several months earlier and hoped to meet someone new.

I avoided online dating for a long time, because my brother had a horrible experience with it, and, frankly, the crazies you hear about completely terrified me.

On the other hand, my friend Carol met her husband online and he is wonderful. Waffling over the idea, I understood that if I wanted to post a profile, I needed to be smart about it. I wouldn't supply any identifying factors about myself. No real name, no specific address, no pictures of my house or kids. Unsure what type of men I would encounter online, I tried to keep an open mind. Stories circulated how the men online only looked for sex or weren't forthcoming in revealing their relationship status with other women. I had to be careful. I hoped to meet genuine men, weeded out from the ones who simply wanted to hook up.

Plenty of dating sites exist. Some are free and some charge upwards of $200 a year. Two hundred dollars seemed expensive to me, but my wise friend Kelly said, "No guy will pay that much if he isn't serious about meeting someone, right?" But I still wasn't ready to drop $200.

My friend Lynn tried online dating too, so we shared our concerns. She was ready to meet someone, but similarly hesitant. At dinner with our friend Kristin, Lynn updated us on her search. She had been anonymously talking to a couple of men because they didn't post a photo. She then confessed that she didn't have a picture of herself on the site. Kristin said, "Think about it like this: when you're house hunting and looking at realtors' websites, you want to view a picture of the house, right? You will pass on a house if you don't know what it looks like." Good point. But if you don't post a picture and you truly connect with someone, are looks a high priority? Something to ponder...

Finally ready, I filled out the basic questionnaire on Plenty of Fish, uploaded a few photos, and gave myself a pseudonym because I wanted to be anonymous and safe. That wasn't so bad. The toughest part was describing myself without going into a ton of details or sounding arrogant, but still come across as witty and interesting. And besides, who wants to brag about themselves? Some of the guys on the site copped out and said "Ask me" without saying anything about themselves. Pass.

I'm no grammar Nazi, but bios that contained sentences that started with lower case letters, lower case "i", and abbreviated words like "ur" and "plz" irritated the hell out of me. If I wanted to correspond with someone like that, I'd talk to a 12-year-old. Show me that you are an adult and can write like one.

A self-professed talker, I find it difficult to carry on a conversation with someone who isn't as outgoing as me. These men on the site were strangers to me, so I needed to come up with a way to initiate real dialog with them. In my profile, I wrote, "If you decide to message me, please don't write 'Hi' or 'Hey', because I won't write back. Ask me an open-ended question or two, so we can learn more about each other." Don't waste my time by not reading my profile.

Within a minute of hitting the Publish My Profile button, two men sent me messages. Were they online trolling for new fish or did they like what they read about me? In my optimism, I wanted to think the latter. Regardless, my ego immediately skyrocketed.

Twenty-four hours later, 10 more men contacted me. A couple of them only wrote "Hi" or "Hey" and were immediately deleted. Obviously, they only scoped out my pictures and didn't read my bio. I received a message from a 24-year-old who said he wanted me. Flattered, but I told him he was way too young for me. He seemed undeterred, but I didn't reply.

The remaining men took the time to read my profile and asked me specific questions about it. One wrote, "Great to see that you are a Steelers and Penguins fan." (I'm a Pittsburgh girl.) Another wrote, "How was your day?" I'm sure he didn't want to hear about the boring stuff I did all day, like running my kids to basketball practice and work meetings, but I appreciated that he asked an open-ended question. Being the friendly person that I am, I replied to everyone.

The next day, 10 more men contacted me. I weeded out the "Hi" and "Hey" messages again and replied to the new messages. But by this time, the first group of men had responded to me and now I had 15 different men talking to me. One of those original men wrote, "I'd like to get to know you better", gave me his cell number, and told me to call him. Whoa. At this point, I was not ready to disclose my real name or phone number to anyone. And how did he assume I wasn't a sociopath? How could he trust me so quickly without learning anything about me?

Later the second day, I received a message from a new guy. Even though he listed his first name in his profile, I'll call him The Biker since he posted a picture of himself riding a bicycle. (Many other men listed their first names, proving a noticeable difference in safety concerns between men and women on the site.) The Biker told me that he liked what I wrote in my profile and said it resonated with him. Hmmm.... he used a big word. I liked this guy already. He asked me several open-ended questions and told me a little bit about himself. He was my age, had a daughter, and lived about 25 miles from me. He had traveled a lot, like I did, and he liked cooking good food. I could already comprehend that we would have lots to talk about. Immediately, I replied and answered all of his questions. The Biker topped my list of most compatible matches on the site.

On the third day, 10 more men contacted me, plus I had replies from the first and second days. Was I that popular or did more men than women have profiles on the site? Flattered by all of the attention, but I had no idea how to weed men out. I wanted to be nice to everyone and not disappear, but I felt overwhelmed. I got another message from The Biker and found out more about him. He asked me my name, saying he wanted to make sure I was a real person. Although intrigued, I still couldn't bring myself to disclose my name. Not ready, I assured him that I was indeed real, but I wanted to be safe. He said he understood.

On the fourth day, I immediately logged on to the dating site as soon as I got home from work. Ten more messages. Add the replies from almost everyone from the previous days. Forty messages. Feeling inundated, I couldn't keep up. I felt bad that I couldn't reply to everyone as fast as I could and found myself becoming a slave to the site. That wasn't me. Not at all. I had a life. Before this, I could go a week without turning on my laptop. The rush of reading who replied to me and how quickly they would do it hooked me.

I still liked hearing from The Biker and even told him that my first name started with "M." Baby steps.

On the fifth day, I finally reached capacity. I realized I became addicted to the site and got an adrenaline rush from all the attention. None of these men knew me and I struggled opening myself up to strangers so quickly. I was so overwhelmed that I had no idea how to pick and choose the best man for me. The Biker had the only fighting chance. Nevertheless, I decided to take down my profile. But before I did, I contacted The Biker one last time and told him that I was besieged with everything and that I was deactivating my account.

I told him he was the only one who interested me. I took a deep breath and gave him my first name. I also told him that if he wanted to meet me, he could reach me by text, and gave him my phone number. My heart pounded when I gave out that info, but this was my only shot to talk to him again. I clicked Send and waited a few hours for The Biker to respond.

When I checked my messages later that night, no message from The Biker. But in my message to him, my phone number was not in the body of the email. I wondered if the site recognized the digits and deleted them as per their safety rules? (But how did that other guy send me his phone number?) I didn't have it in me to keep my profile up, so I deleted it. The Biker was gone.

I chose to disable my account and sever ties with The Biker, but I wondered what it would have been like to meet him in person. Maybe we would have hit it off? Or maybe he didn't want to deal with a lunatic who freaked out about online dating after five days?

Lesson #4: Be smart about online dating, so that you have less of a chance of the creeps finding you.

Chapter 5

The next Bachelorette

I'm not a big fan of reality TV, but occasionally, I'd catch a glimpse of *The Bachelorette* (Rachel Lindsey is my favorite) and watch the girl in the driver's seat of finding love. My daughter and I watched an entire season when one of the guys from the next town over appeared on the show and we rooted for him. (One night, he sat right behind me at my son's soccer game because he was scouting for his team.) How realistic is it that someone could think that they could find love and get engaged in three months? Sure, she weeded out suitors, but to find serious love in that short amount of time seemed improbable to me.

Despite my cynicism, several of my friends (girls and guys) told me that I would make a great bachelorette. My first reaction was that I wouldn't want the entire nation to watch me get my heart broken on TV. But then again, someone could unexpectedly dump me at any time and I'd be sad regardless. I looked into it and read the fine print rules on the website. Turns out I can't qualify because my younger brother works for Disney and immediate relatives are ineligible to participate.

Not deterred, I had another idea. I would date around like the girl on the show and select potential suitors. Unfortunately, I didn't have a pool of random eligible bachelors at my disposal or free trips to Europe. Putting online dating on the back burner, I had to come up with another option. Then I remembered my great friends. They had to know somebody, didn't they? And they could vouch for someone to alleviate my fear of meeting a serial killer. I wanted to ask them without sounding desperate, so I came up with an email to use:

The new bachelorette...that would be me!

Instead of going on that show, I am taking a different course of action. Things didn't work out with (insert latest guy's name here) and a wise person told me, "Long term, you'll be glad to not be with someone who didn't realize how awesome you are." I am back on the market. And who, besides my awesome friends like you, can help me find someone great? I am putting myself in your hands... Maybe you know a single guy who you think would like to meet me. Maybe your brother, your cousin, your coworker, or your coworker's cousin.

A lot of you have been friends with me for a long time, so you understand what kind of person I am, but here is what I am looking for in someone else. You all learned that I can support myself, so I don't need anyone to take care of me. I'd like to find someone to spend time with and do things with, someone who can show me some attention, and have an intelligent conversation. Someone who opens the car door for me.

Here are my must-haves:

-He must be a non-smoker.

-He must like kids and want to be around them.

-He must have a full-time job and be able to support himself.

-He must live by himself (or with his kids).

-He must keep his house fairly clean. I don't want to run from there screaming!

Here are my "nice to haves":

-His age should be 38-50.

-He should live within 20 miles of me.

-He should like dogs.

-He should be active and like to get up and do things.

-He should have a pretty good attitude about life.

You all can't predict if I'll have chemistry with this person, so that's my job to get out and meet him. We can start by getting lunch or drinks, so we can learn more about each other. For one, we'll have you in common.

Think about the single men in your life, get in contact with him, and then mention me to him. I trust your approval process.

Here is to a new chapter in my life - and thank you for being such an awesome friend!

This idea is worth a shot, right? If I'm not promoting myself, then who is?

Lesson #5: Enlist your friends to help you find someone.

Chapter 6

Off-Limits

Married men have continuously hit on me in the past 20+ years. The first time it happened was while I worked as a waitress at a country club on summer break from college. I never learned the man's age, but he was married and had children older than me. At the time, he seemed *old*. I wondered if he had any respect for his wife if he flirted with a girl young enough to be his daughter.

These days, married men still ogle and flirt with me. I don't know what is going on inside their marriage for them to think that I might be interested in them, but I am not about to find out. Maybe they are natural flirts and have no further interest in me? Maybe their wife lost interest in them? Maybe they don't find her attractive anymore? Maybe they like the hunt for off-limit, fresh meat? Regardless of the answer, I told them I was flattered and politely declined.

Several years ago, a male co-worker of mine found out that I had recently left my ex-husband and started flirting with me. I had met his stunning wife a couple of times. Did he need something new and different? He told me that they had an open marriage and that she would agree if he and I fooled around. I had heard about open marriages but never knew someone in one. Intrigued, but I wondered that he might not be forthcoming. I didn't want to hook up with him, only to have her come after me. Women can be vicious when they discover someone is after their man, even if they aren't paying any attention to him. I graciously refused. In hindsight, maybe I should have called his bluff for fun?

Another married co-worker of mine told me about a sensual dream he had about me and that he fantasized about me while doing the deed with his wife. Whoa! What did he expect me to say to that?

A man I knew who had a girlfriend sent me a message through Facebook, saying, "if circumstances were different, I would have asked you out." I didn't respond. I have no desire to get involved with someone who is dating another woman. Besides, I don't try out.

One night, I was out with my girlfriends Kelly and Michele listening to a band. Kelly started talking to this guy and he offered to buy us all a drink. The ring on his left hand confirmed his marital status and I politely declined. I wasn't comfortable accepting a drink from a married man. Kelly and Michele both razzed me about it, saying it was only a drink.

On the other end of the spectrum, I don't cheat. Once I am in a committed relationship, that's something I don't do. I haven't had the situation yet, but I have to think if I meet someone else, I hope to have the decency to end the first relationship before starting things up with the second person. That's the right thing to do.

If I am in an exclusive relationship, I won't give out my phone number to someone who likes me, because I don't even want to be tempted to flirt with someone else. Besides the obvious moral reasons, fooling around is way too stressful. Besides, in this day and age, with Facebook and cell phone tracking, it's easy to get caught cheating. Why put yourself through that? If reasons exist to cheat, then the relationship has flaws and I don't want to be in it. Do everyone a favor and end it.

Everyone has their idea of what constitutes cheating. If a guy is at a strip club (and his girlfriend/wife is fully aware that he is there), and he is looking and not touching, I don't consider that cheating. The stripper will not jump off the stage and fondle him. However, he should NOT get a private lap dance.

Women don't have the same circumstances. While in Cancun several years ago on a girls' trip, I had started seeing someone and didn't intend to hook up with anyone else. One night, I talked with some people at the bar and stepped away to call my kids. When I got off the phone, this engaged man I met the night before came up to me and started talking to me. He flirted heavily with me, but I kept my distance. He then stepped closer to me and put his hand on my chest and felt up my girls. Taken aback and completely horrified, I froze in place. In hindsight, I should have slugged him. I don't consider this cheating on my part, because I didn't invite the groping. He, on the other hand, was completely out of line and I felt bad for his fiancée.

Here's what I think about cheating. If you are kissing/sexting/groping/telling someone you love them who isn't your significant other, then it's cheating. Period.

Lesson #6: It's never a good idea to get involved with someone who is already in an exclusive relationship. Stay away.

Chapter 7

The Professor

Now that you learned more about me and what I think, I can tell you more about my experiences meeting men. I've met some great guys and some real douchebags. I've learned a lot from each one and hope to learn more as time goes on. I know what I don't want, but I am still learning what I do want.

Let's start with The Professor.

I went to high school with The Professor. We went on a few casual dates back then and he was always a teenage crush of mine. He graduated with my older brother and we lost touch for a couple of years. During my freshman year in college, I walked back to my dorm one afternoon between classes and work when I found The Professor sitting on a bench outside my dorm. How did he find me? (After all, Google didn't exist back then.) He told me his college debate team was on campus and he looked me up at the Info Desk.

After chatting with him for 20 minutes, I told him I was on my way to work, so I couldn't stick around. I opted not to tell him that I had a boyfriend (who would later be my ex-husband) and wished him good luck with his debate team.

Jump ahead 18 years...

Soon after I left my husband, I visited my older brother and we had fun going through his Facebook friends, talking about our former classmates and what they did now. The Professor was one of my brother's friends and he suggested I send The Professor a friend request. I balked at the thought, doubting that The Professor would remember me because too much time had passed. "Just do it," my brother pushed. I finally caved (big brothers can be like that...) and sent The Professor a friend request. To my surprise, he accepted it within a couple of days.

Over the next few months, The Professor and I exchanged emails every few days and caught up on what had been happening in our lives over the past 18 years. I gave him an abridged version of why I left my ex-husband and told him about my job and my kids. He told me that he lived six states away, had never been married, and considered his students to be his kids. His parents had retired to Arizona, but he still had family in our hometown. He kept me laughing with his wit and I remembered why I had such a crush on him years earlier. He told me that he often went back home during summer breaks to visit friends and family.

Then I received a wedding invitation from a friend back home. I held my breath, took the plunge, and asked The Professor if he wanted to be my +1. My nerves kicked in asking him to accompany me, as this would be my first real date since I'd left my husband six months before.

The Professor said, "I would LOVE to be your arm candy, but I already have plans to go to Arizona to be with my parents. My dad has cancer. If you want, why don't you come out to Arizona sometime this summer and visit me?" Was he serious? Did he realize what he asked me? I hadn't seen him in 18 years, so what did he anticipate from me? Did he expect sex? My friend Denise gave me some solid advice. She said, "Just do your girl thing and let him make the first move."

I had never been to Arizona before. So many thoughts ran through my mind. After weighing my options for almost a week, I decided yes, I would take a trip to Arizona to visit him. If nothing else, I needed to take a trip by myself and get away from the drama of my divorce. But I had a backup plan. Fortunately, my friend Niki lived in Arizona at the time and, if anything went south with The Professor, I had an alternate plan to bunk on her couch.

I worried for nothing. The trip was amazing! The Professor and I went hiking, explored Flagstaff and the Grand Canyon, had a lot of fun catching up, and ate great food. He was a complete gentleman, too. When we checked into the hotel on the first night, he asked the clerk to get us a rollaway bed, because the room only had one bed. Mysteriously, the extra bed never came. I joked with him for a long time afterward that he went back and slipped the desk clerk $20 not to bring the bed up.

On the last day of my trip, we talked about how we wanted to see each other again but understood the difficulty of being separated by six states. He stayed in Arizona to visit more with his parents and I traveled back home.

Three weeks later, he left Arizona by train to come back East and asked me to meet him in New Orleans. I jumped at the chance. I hadn't been to New Orleans since childhood and couldn't wait to explore the city with him as an adult.

While in New Orleans, The Professor sheepishly confessed that he didn't do his own laundry. I gave him a funny look when he told me. What adult doesn't do their own laundry? He sent his out to a laundry service. That should have been my first red flag.

Over the next few months, The Professor and I talked to each other daily and we met up in October and November that year. I didn't consider him my boyfriend yet, so I went on occasional dates with other people.

At Christmas, I sent him a photo book of us together in Arizona and New Orleans and a button-down shirt. I hoped to get something back from him before he went to Arizona again to visit his parents. Nothing. I called him after New Year's and asked if he got my package. He had. I was so hurt that he hadn't sent me anything or even acknowledged that I'd sent him a Christmas gift. Red flag #2...

I forgave The Professor for the lack of a Christmas present and, by spring, we were in an exclusive relationship. We'd get together once a month over the next three years and talk several times a day. In the beginning, our relationship was good. We'd laugh and share things and send each other things in the mail. I fell for him.

The Professor helped me experience a lot of things that I might not have done on my own. We traveled to Charleston, Hawaii, Arizona a couple more times, and Annapolis. We watched live music in hole-in-the-wall clubs and sampled a lot of great food. I will always be thankful to him for doing new things.

At the 18-month mark, I insisted that The Professor meet my kids. He had been avoiding them for a long time and insisted that my divorce be finalized before he met them. (My ex-husband dragged my divorce out for 3-1/2 years.) One did not preclude the other. I told The Professor that if he didn't meet my kids, then I would break up with him. I'm not one to offer ultimatums, but I had waited long enough, put up with his nonsense, and felt justified. Red flag #3....

He got annoyed with me a few times when I didn't tell him that I hung out with my guy friends. Then, he questioned all of my male Facebook friends, growled at me when I mentioned a male friend's name, and often called me every five minutes until he got a hold of me. But he flat out refused to introduce me to his female friends. He constantly pressured me to chop my long hair and wear frumpy clothes. He frequently boasted what a great catch he was. He also refused to go to my parents' 40th-anniversary party, three weddings, my nephew's baptism, my family reunion, and vacations with my kids. As time went on, I learned that his insane jealousy, needs, and insecurity took the forefront of his personality. Red flag #4...

After dating for three years, he had promised me for 18 months that he wanted to move to be with my kids and me. Then he got a fantastic offer from Clemson University to teach for a year. I told him that he needed to take the job. Fearful that I would break up with him, I told him to give me a reason to wait. His idea of a "reason to wait" was a promise ring pledging to move the following year to be with me. Hadn't he assured me that already for the past 18 months? He couldn't even utter the words that he wanted to marry me. When he presented me with the ring, I blurted, "Don't you think we are too old for promise rings?" (Yes, I was harsh, but come on....) I was so disappointed. I attempted to get over my hesitation about getting married again, but what was his reason? Red flag #5...

I wanted so badly for the relationship to work that I ignored the red flags.

The following month, we took my kids to Boston for vacation. This trip was our first family trip together because The Professor found ways to avoid my kids. Red flag #6...

Several weeks later, he frantically tried to get things done for his new job at Clemson because he never planned ahead. He sent me an unwarranted nasty text saying that the vacation must've worked out well for me, but didn't end up fitting into his schedule.

By this time, I had had enough. He had pushed me to my limit and I was exhausted being with him. I wanted to throw my car at him in anger. I needed to calm down, so I didn't respond to his text. A couple of hours later, he called and apologized profusely for what he had said. I forgave him but discerned that it would be the only time that I would exonerate him for talking badly about being around my children. We were a package deal, I reminded him.

A few weeks later, he sent me another unjustified text, saying that I needed to show him more care when he was under so much stress. What was I, his mother? I was livid! He didn't own a home or have kids, and notoriously didn't pay his bills on time. He had no idea how to be a responsible adult. I didn't speak to him for 10 days.

Then, on the 10th day, he sent me an onslaught of malicious texts, cursing at me, calling me "F*cking trash" and accusing me of sleeping around. He was so far over the edge that I didn't respond to any of it. I could not out-crazy crazy.

The next day, I told him he could go to hell and completely cut him out of my life. I blocked his email, phone number, and Facebook account. I forgot to block him from my work email and he sent me an offensive email insisting that I apologize to him for ignoring him. Before I blocked him at work, I emailed him back saying that I had nothing to apologize for and that he needed to grow up. I was done.

The next couple of weeks were marred with anger and tears. I couldn't believe he was so entitled that he thought he could be so vicious.

Three months went by...

Just before Christmas, The Professor sent me a box containing a six-page montage of photos of us, several small gifts, and a letter apologizing that he hadn't spent more time with my kids, and never proposed. He also included 53 future birthday cards. I guessed the random number of cards because I was 40 when this happened and I always told him that my Grandma lived to be 93 and I hoped to live as long as she did, so 40 + 53 = 93. He never once apologized for the cruel texts that he sent me. The package was heartfelt, but I only wanted an apology for how he had treated me. I didn't want any of the gifts and donated them all to the local women's shelter.

A couple of days later, The Professor created a new email account and asked me if I received the package. I told him I did but reprimanded him that I didn't get an apology from him for the way he spoke to me. I didn't hear back from him.

Eight months went by...

One afternoon at work, an email appeared in my Inbox from The Professor. I think I dropped the F-Bomb a few times when I read it. The first sentence said, "For the record, I do apologize for what I said to you." I finally got my apology. The Professor stated that he was in town and asked about my availability that night. Was he joking? Did he think that I had no self-respect? I had zero interest in meeting him.

I cursed The Professor to my friend Allan and he told me I needed to meet The Professor. "Why?" I balked. Allan explained that sometime down the road, I might realize that I had the opportunity to hear out The Professor and get the apology that I wanted, and I would kick myself if I didn't take it. Allan was right and I conceded.

I met The Professor later that night for a drink and suspiciously asked him why he came to town. He explained to me that he talked to a local college about a job that came up and wanted to rekindle our relationship. Speechless for a moment, I told him I had moved on and that I couldn't go back to what we had. I explained that I forgave him, but didn't trust him not to do it again. Unsure if we could be friends like he wanted, I told him not to push me. I had to catch myself to not be snarky with him. Even though he didn't deserve my kindness, I wanted to be the bigger person.

Allan was right. Thankful for some closure, I did not envision The Professor in my future. That crushing feeling finally came where I admitted to myself that this relationship was over.

Lesson #7: Don't ignore red flags. Save yourself from the later grief.

Chapter 8

The Veteran

Two weeks after I ended things with The Professor, I met The Veteran through Allan and some other friends. I know, I know, only two weeks had passed, and I was still reeling, but hear me out... Tired of feeling sorry for myself, my friends insisted on taking me out to cheer me up. I had no expectations to meet anyone, but I needed to get out of my house and do something fun for myself. My dog probably wanted time to herself, too.

Since I had no intentions of meeting anyone that night, I had nothing to lose. No chance of rejection. No letdowns. Nothing. I didn't care if I went home by myself that night. However, I had a little too much to drink and was too intoxicated to drive home when everyone called it a night. The Veteran witnessed my hesitation at the bar and offered to stay with me for a while after everyone else left.

After 20 minutes, The Veteran asked me if I wanted to leave the bar. Still unable to drive, I asked if a late-night diner was nearby that we could walk to. He sheepishly said that he lived a mile away and that I could sober up at his place if I wanted. Whoa. I had met this guy mere hours before. He was one of Allan's best friends, but that's all I knew about him. The Veteran seemed sincere and concerned about my well-being and professed his honorable intentions. He insisted that he would bring me back to my car once I sobered up. I took the plunge and surmised that if anything bad happened, Allan would hear about it.

When we arrived at The Veteran's house, he immediately got me a glass of water. His place was mostly neat and clean. I noticed a couple of pictures of a little girl on the wall. When I narrowed my drunken eyes and looked closer, I read the label of "Goddaughter" on the picture frame. He liked kids but didn't have any of his own. Point for him.

The Veteran led me to his couch, we sat down and talked for a little bit. Maybe the extra liquor boosted my imagination, but this guy hung on my every word. My knees pressed up against his and I apologized for invading his personal space. He said, "That's okay" and kissed me. I immediately sobered up!

We made out like teenagers for the next two hours. I wasn't about to sleep with someone I just met (more on that later), so we stayed at first base. He flirted with me and talked intimately with me, inches from my face. My face warmed as he spoke so close to me. After a while, the clock on his TV read 2:00 in the morning. Part of me wanted to stay longer, but the part of me making him want more won out. I told The Veteran that I needed to go and he drove me back to my car. He insisted that I tell him that I got home in one piece and gave me his number so that I could text him.

Twenty minutes later, safe at home, I sent him a text saying that I had a great time. He sent me a text back saying the same and wished me sweet dreams.

The next day, The Veteran called me and we talked for an hour. This guy was smart and funny and I could tell he enjoyed life. Over the next two days, we constantly emailed, texted, and talked on the phone when we could. We talked about our jobs, cooking our favorite dishes, our similar backgrounds, our love of books, and our favorite hole-in-the-wall restaurants. He promised to give me a personal tour of his library and lend me any books that I wanted to borrow. He was surprised to learn that I had guessed that he had sleep apnea because he was a veteran. (My brother, who is a Navy vet, told me that most people in the military have sleep apnea because of their abnormal schedules.) The Veteran told me that not many non-military folks are aware of that.

I told The Veteran that I needed to buy a new door lock at Home Depot and asked him if he wanted to meet me there the next day and go out for dinner afterward. He replied, "A hot girl at a hardware store - what could be better?"

When I met The Veteran at Home Depot the next night, he pulled me into his arms and kissed me sweetly on the mouth, as if he had done it a thousand times. I blushed. This guy was dreamy. Brain *and* brawn.

After we left Home Depot, we got dinner at a nearby restaurant. The waitress took our order and The Veteran requested oil and vinegar on his salad. He then got up to use the restroom. While he was gone, the waitress came back and asked me, "Does he want balsamic vinegar or raspberry vinegar?" I giggled and said, "I don't know.... it's our first date!" She chuckled and said she would bring both.

After dinner, we said our goodbyes and we set up a date in a few days on the weekend. The beginning of our relationship happened too fast and too soon for me, but I was smitten. I hoped it wasn't all in my head. Over the next two days, we continued the constant contact... all day, every day. The Veteran sent me a text when he got up in the morning, wishing me a great day. And he sent me a sweet dreams text when he went to bed. He even told me he would watch snail races with me. I was tickled that he wanted to do the most mundane thing with me because he simply wanted to be with me.

I also feared that he was falling too fast and too soon. We had known each other less than a week, but I decided to keep that concern to myself. His intellect and emotions matched mine and I looked forward to more.

But on Saturday morning, things drastically changed. By noon, I hadn't heard from The Veteran at all, against his usual M.O. I texted him asking if everything was okay. Without going into detail, he said he was experiencing multiple personal issues and needed to take care of things. Okay, no problem. Everyone gets issues. I told him to do what he needed to do and that I could wait.

Over the next two weeks, I only got a couple of choppy, vague texts from The Veteran. I had no idea what was going on but was hurt that he disappeared without much explanation. I honestly felt that we had clicked. Curious about what happened, but I resisted the temptation to go to his house, demanding answers. Over the next month, I sent The Veteran a couple more texts to find out how he was doing. He never gave me the courtesy of a response. Done waiting for him, I deleted him from my phone.

I later learned that The Veteran had some serious PTSD issues; hence, his disappearance. At that time in my life, I was in no shape to help him. I needed to, for lack of better words, get my own shit together first. Hopefully, he did too.

Lesson #8: If someone disappears on you, don't hunt them down demanding answers. It's almost always not about you.

Chapter 9

Alone for the Holidays

Some people are afraid and depressed at the thought of being alone on Christmas. I looked forward to it. My kids were with their dad and all of my family lives out of state. Because of the short holiday break, I couldn't travel to be with them. I was completely alone. I told a few of my friends that I would be by myself, but not because I wanted their pity. Reassuring them that I would not wallow in my misery, I would come out a better person having spent the holiday without a man.

My friend Carol and her husband still insisted that I have Christmas Eve dinner with them. They understood that I didn't need a man, but still wanted to spread the Christmas spirit with me and enjoy a good meal. I couldn't pass up the invitation and spent Christmas Eve with them. After dinner, I stopped at another friend's house before heading to Christmas Eve Mass on my own.

(My mother is Italian and my father is Irish. How can I not be Catholic?)

Mass was full of dressed-up families singing carols. I didn't mind standing by myself and didn't even notice if people could tell that I was alone. How many people come to Christmas Eve Mass by themselves? I'm sure I could count on one hand. In a space where everyone communed for the same purpose, I was calm and content. I couldn't predict my future, but I was fine not knowing.

After Mass, I went home to my dog and slept well that night. Who says being alone on Christmas is a bad thing? I had my kids, my family, and my friends, so what made one particular day the determining factor of whether or not I was lonely? Did I want to be like this for 10 years? Probably not. But I could get through a few years like this.

Lesson #9: Spend time by yourself.

Chapter 10

The Volleyball Player

On the last day that I tried online dating, I received an odd message. Like I said earlier, I didn't use my real name online, so I apprehensively read the message starting with, "Mary, is that you?" Who was this person and how did he recognize me? He explained that we used to work together eight years ago and wondered if I remembered him.

The Volleyball Player immediately asked me out for drinks, so we could catch up. When I initially agreed (after all, what harm could drinks do?), he told me that he already had plans with his friends that Saturday and asked if I wanted to join them. I hadn't talked to this guy in eight years and he wanted to get reacquainted with his friends around? That didn't sound like a real date to me. Hesitant to commit, I conveyed that I would let him know.

That Friday night, I caught an early movie by myself. After the movie, I arranged to meet my friend Cathy and her husband at a pub on the same block. In between raindrops, I rushed over to the bar, only to find Cathy and her hubby gone. I didn't want to walk outside in the rain, so I waited a few minutes inside the pub and called my kids before I headed home.

The rain let up and I decided to make a break for it. The downpour cleared the sidewalks except for one man walking toward me. I walked past him and didn't think much of him. Then I heard "Mary?" and immediately turned my head. The Volleyball Player stood a few feet from me. Had I not taken those extra few minutes inside the bar to call my kids, I would have completely missed him. Someone or something wanted me to be on the sidewalk at that exact moment. (Yes, it sounds like an old John Cusack movie, but I swear that's what happened.)

The Volleyball Player told me he was on his way to meet a friend at the pub I had left. Did I want to join him, he asked. No time to analyze, I said yes. After all, if the night soured, I could easily excuse myself and decline the next night's dinner date. We walked back to the bar, met his friend, and The Volleyball Player bought me a gin and tonic.

Over a couple of drinks, I got reacquainted with The Volleyball Player. He had been single for a few years, played volleyball in a men's league, coached his son's little league baseball team, led his son's scout troop, and camped and hiked a lot. More of a city slicker myself, I listened with an open mind. By midnight, I wanted to go home and asked The Volleyball Player to walk me to my car. When he did, he asked me again about going out the next night. This time, he suggested we could get dinner on our own first, and then meet up with his friends. That idea sounded better to me and I agreed.

The Volleyball Player and I went out on several more dates after that. He kept himself fit and he dressed well. He kept a clean house, had some basic cooking skills, liked his job, and seemed to be a great dad, even though I hadn't met his young son. Our custody schedules overlapped, so we could only have a date every other weekend and sometimes an occasional lunch during the week.

Despite being cordial to me, The Volleyball Player didn't go out of his way for me. When we went hiking, he walked 10 steps ahead of me and not with me. Whenever I cooked for us, he didn't bring a bottle of wine (or even beer) to my house for us to share. Whenever we went somewhere, he never opened the car door for me. (I learned from him not to be a "chirp-chirp girl.") He rarely kissed me when he first saw me – not even on the cheek.

The final oddity came when he told me he was playing volleyball with his teammates and I asked him if I could attend. He replied, "I'll let you know when the time is right for you to come watch." I understood keeping our kids out of the picture until we were both ready, but I didn't understand why he didn't want me to watch him play volleyball. Was it that private to him? Was someone else at volleyball who he didn't want me to meet? I didn't understand how to respond to his aloofness. How did he expect to learn more about someone if he didn't let her in his life? Annoyed that he shut me out, I told him that I would make other plans.

At the two-month mark, The Volleyball Player invited me to come over and take a dip in his hot tub. I put on my skimpiest bikini and hoped that he would notice. Nope. Nothing. He barely kissed me in the hot tub. The Volleyball Player didn't shower me with compliments all the time, but come on... throw me a little bone. I wanted more attention than I got and dating him seemed more trouble than what it was worth. With our odd schedules, we barely had enough time together as it was.

After I left that evening, I got a text from The Volleyball Player. He wrote, "You looked HOT in that bikini!" Why didn't he say something earlier? He had his opportunity and he blew it. I wanted more from The Volleyball Player and he wasn't giving it to me. I had paid my dues with the long-distance romance with The Professor and I didn't want to go through that again. The Volleyball Player lived 20 minutes from me, but I was frustrated that we didn't get together often. He seemed to keep me at arm's length and didn't make me a priority.

The following week, The Volleyball Player called me and said he didn't think that we should date each other anymore. He maintained that we didn't have enough chemistry. (I had other ideas that I won't disclose.) Not heartbroken, I didn't cry or get upset. The conversation blew my ego more than anything else, as I had hoped to end it with him first. I appreciated that he was mature enough to tell me that he didn't want to see me again; he hadn't cowardly disappeared. He hoped we could still do things as friends, but I didn't need another male friend. I didn't hear from him again – even though he continually "Liked" my occasional Facebook postings.

Lesson #10:   If someone can't show you some common courtesy, affection, or passion in a relationship, it's best to walk away.

Chapter 11

The Usher

Through a mutual friend, I first met The Usher a good 15 years ago. Ten years later, I ran into him at a book conference where I hawked my first book. He attended the conference to meet the keynote speaker, David Baldacci. We didn't run into each other again for a year or so after.

Then, when I changed churches, I discovered that The Usher always worked the 11 a.m. Mass at my new church. I don't remember exactly when it started, but whenever The Usher saw me (sometimes in the back of the church), he quickly hugged me and kissed me on the cheek. Unsure if he behaved like that with everyone or if he singled me out, I never witnessed him do it to anyone else.

At Mass a couple of weeks before Christmas, I stood in the pew with some space beside me toward the aisle. The Usher came by and leaned into me. I assumed he was trying to hug me again, so I slanted toward him and kissed him on the cheek. Nope, that's not what he was doing and my face turned 16 shades of red. He was simply doing his job as an usher and asked if I could scoot over more, so he could seat some latecomers. Oops.

At the end of Christmas Eve Mass, The Usher and I chatted for a few minutes. He then said to me, "You know, we should talk outside of church," but didn't ask for my phone number at that time. I went to Mass the following week and talked with The Usher again, but he still didn't attempt to exchange contact information. Almost sure he was single (and not gay), I didn't understand why he dragged things out. I finally took matters into my own hands the following week and handed him a piece of paper with my email and phone number on it.

A week went by and I didn't hear anything from The Usher. Finally, that Saturday night I went out on my first date with The Volleyball Player (and his friends), and my phone rang. Not recognizing the number, I clicked my phone to end the call. My phone immediately rang again from the same number. I excused myself from the conversation with The Volleyball Player and took the phone call, thinking it was a wrong number, so I could tell the person on the other line they had made a mistake. Nope, The Usher called me. How awkward to be on a date with one guy and talking to another. I quickly told The Usher that I was out with friends and could barely hear him (it was kind of the truth...) and that I would call him back the next day.

Over the next couple of months, The Usher and I reached out to each other several times a week and I saw him every Sunday. His texts spanned several sentences long, talking about his day or asking about mine, and he almost always sent smiley faces or winks. His behavior seemed like he was into me, but he still didn't ask me out. I didn't get it. I liked that The Usher was a super nice guy and upstanding. He made sure an elderly woman made it to church every week when she could no longer drive.

A week after The Volleyball Player ended things with me, I lamented to Allan about The Usher. I needed a man's opinion because nothing made sense to me or any of my girlfriends. Allan had a plan. He said, "Invite The Usher over for dinner with your kids. Keep it low key, say that you'll have plenty of food and that you'd love it if he can join you. That way, it's not a real date, but it will allow him to ask you out afterward." Sounded like a good idea to me.

My casual dinner with The Usher went well. He even brought cookies for our dessert. Unfortunately, Allan's foolproof plan had failed. The Usher did not ask me out, even though we continued to talk a couple of times a week. He was kind, but he mystified me.

Six weeks later, The Usher texted me around 10:30 p.m., asking me about my day. I said, "I had a great day and my friend Denise even bought me a bottle of wine for my birthday." The Usher replied, "Today is your birthday?" I confirmed that it was. Then The Usher said, "We should go out right now, so I can buy you a drink for your birthday." Was he finally asking me out? Unfortunately, I had to decline because my kids were with me for the week. I told The Usher that I would take a rain check.

A month later, one of The Usher's closest friends unexpectedly passed away and he was completely grief-stricken. I had met his friend a handful of times several years earlier. The Usher said he needed to get out and get a beer and asked if I would join him and let him finally buy me the birthday drink he had promised. I met The Usher for an hour that night and he vented about his friend. I was there for him and I hope he appreciated it. But I realized that night that The Usher and I didn't have a spark.

Nine months went by and The Usher and I talked several times a week. He never once asked me out. Instead, he helped me move heavy things around my house and I helped him shop for a new laptop. One morning right before church, The Usher saw me in the parking lot and came up to me and put his arm around me. If anyone watched us, they might have assumed we were a couple. The Usher had no problem being touchy-feely with me. I still didn't get his intentions, but it's best that The Usher and I never dated.

He was genuinely nice, but if he couldn't take the lead and ask me out, then I needed to find someone who would. I didn't want to be the one to carry the relationship. He still kisses me on the cheek every time he sees me, even though we'll always be friends.

Lesson #11: If a man is slow to step up and make the first move to ask a girl out, he never will.

Chapter 12

Sex

I've never had sex with someone the same night I have met them. Some women don't think anything is wrong with it, but, in my mind, a man needs to earn the right before I have sex with him. And who came up with the idea of making three dates the threshold for sex? Was it someone with xy chromosomes? I barely know a man at three dates, so I sure as hell don't want to be naked with the guy.

If a guy treats you like he doesn't care about you, then do not make excuses for him and DO NOT reward him with sex. We women sometimes get caught up on someone who pays us the slightest bit of attention, because we don't want to be alone. But we forget how awesome we are. We don't need a man to validate that. We need a man to be our partner and supporter, not someone who only wants a 3 a.m. hookup.

Once a woman has sex with a man, what does she have left in her arsenal? These women forget that we hold all the cards. The late, great Robin Williams declared, "God gave men a penis and a brain, but only enough blood to pump one at a time." We women need to use that to our advantage.

A woman has a lot of power over a man when she doesn't have sex with him. Why give the man all the dominance? And why wait around in angst for him to contact us afterward? Why put ourselves through that? He got his bolt of pleasure and is already moving on. Do we even build a foundation of trust if no real relationship exists? If he isn't willing to wait for sex, then we'll be glad in the long run to be rid of him. If he can't fathom that he is with a fabulous, funny, smart, and classy woman, then that is his problem, not ours. We need to find someone who treats us with respect and not as sex objects. Besides, I've never heard a woman say, "Hmmm, I wish we would have had sex on our first date."

My wise friend Paul summed up the whole sex scenario when an acquaintance of ours discovered the hard way that she should not have had sex with a man so freely. He and I witnessed when her sexual partner openly flirted with another woman in front of her and she stormed off.

Paul said, "Sooner or later, a virtuous woman wants commitment; perhaps the other kind don't care, other than commitment-for-the-moment. A casual sex relationship is a bonanza for a man, as he gets what he wants—namely, sex without commitment. For the woman, it's much more problematic, as our acquaintance painfully discovered. She thought she deserved more than sex, but, alas, it was only sex. If her partner prowls this openly in her presence, what's he like when he's out alone?"

That being said, what if we women turned the tables on men? Men seem comfortable in having one-night stands and never contact the woman again. What if women did that? A woman has needs too. Shouldn't a woman get her desires fulfilled without the expectations of having to contact the man again? When that happens, I wonder if the man is then left wanting for more. As a woman, it would be nice to have the upper hand.

When is the best time to take the relationship to the next level? In theory, I'd say don't sleep together until you confirm you are exclusive, but I get that doesn't always happen. Lust blocks out any rational thinking. I've found decent success on the fifth date, but, honestly, I think I should wait later. Two months or more. I'd like to learn more about the guy first before I have sex with him.

And if the man is willing to wait for sex and shows signs that he is interested in you, then he is a keeper!

Conversely, several years ago, I went out with one guy a handful of times. On our first date, he walked me to my door and gentlemanly said goodnight. On the second date, the same thing happened. No kiss. Not even a peck on the cheek. By the fourth date, he still hadn't even attempted to kiss me. I started to think that it was me, questioning his sexual preference. But he continued to ask me out. I appreciated him being a gentleman, but I wanted him to find me attractive, too. He and I are great friends now and he is engaged to someone else who I adore. And they had sex by the fourth date. Now, we joke about what happened, but his peculiarity at the time baffled me.

Lesson #12: Wait for sex.

Chapter 13

The Accountant

I met The Accountant at Denise's birthday party on a cold, windy night in April. When I arrived, I lamented to my friend Kevin that I might be the only single person at the party. Kevin said his long-time, single, friend The Accountant was coming and he had a feeling that we would hit it off. I wanted to find out if he was dating material, so I asked Kevin The Accountant's age. Kevin said 51. Oh. I had never gone out with someone that much older than me. Ten years was a big difference. I feared that The Accountant was balding, overweight, and couldn't keep up with my energy. Kevin reassured me when he showed me a picture of The Accountant and said he biked 40 miles at a time and ran in mini-triathlons. Hell, I didn't even do that, so I pushed aside my concerns about our age difference.

I talked to The Accountant on and off during the party, subtly flirting to show my interest in him. He was low-key, seemed smart and nice. Around 11 p.m., The Accountant gathered his jacket and started saying his goodbyes to everyone. I needed to take matters into my own hands if anything would happen between us, as he'd given no obvious indication that he wanted to ask me out. I quickly grabbed my jacket, said my goodbyes, and followed him out the door to give him the opportunity.

As we walked to our cars, The Accountant asked me if I wanted to go out to dinner sometime. I told him I would like that and he pulled out his phone to add my number. Then I told him to call the number so that I had his number in my phone. He seemed genuinely surprised that I said that. Did someone give him a bogus number in the past? He hugged me and we parted ways. Before I even got home that night, The Accountant sent me a text saying that he was glad we met and hoped that I arrived home safely.

The Accountant and I had our first date 10 days later. I arrived 15 minutes early and grabbed a gin and tonic at the bar. When The Accountant showed up a few minutes later, he sidled up next to me and said to the bartender, "Get me a gin and tonic too." Impressed that he figured out exactly what I drank without even asking me, I inched myself closer to him. Over the next hour, we talked over good food. I learned he had two daughters in their early 20s and had been divorced for 15 years. When we said goodbye later, The Accountant hugged me and quickly kissed me on the cheek. Sweet, I thought. I could go out with him again. He had zero drama and he seemed like a genuinely nice guy.

We made plans the following week to go hiking on the Appalachian Trail. Unlike The Volleyball Player, The Accountant opened my car door then walked alongside me as we hiked. We hiked six miles that day and I didn't even notice that we went that far. When he brought me back to my house, we finally kissed, more than a peck. In a text later that night, he complimented my kissing. How often does someone praise you for your kissing?

On date number four with The Accountant, I invited him to my place to watch his Philadelphia Flyers in the Stanley Cup playoffs. I must've liked the guy to have the Flyers on my TV. (I'm so sorry, my dear Penguins.) We lay on my couch and The Accountant got comfortable with me and rested his hands on my hips. We kissed a few more times, but things remained sweet and intimate.

A few days later, 20 of us went out to celebrate my birthday. I realized The Accountant wouldn't know a lot of my friends. I tried to introduce him to people as I floated around, but I didn't end up doing a good job of it. Near the end of the night, I apologized to him for not being a good hostess. He said not to worry because he didn't need a babysitter. Wow, he wasn't clingy at all and didn't mind meeting new people on his own. Nor did he give me a hard time when I mingled with my male friends (ahem... The Professor).

As we all left the pub, The Accountant walked me to my car, because we had driven separately. While he kissed me, he suggestively asked me what I intended to do next. I replied, feeling high from the party, "Follow me home." The Accountant said, "No, follow me home. I am closer." Up until then, I had never been to The Accountant's house and I wanted a glimpse at how he lived. A week earlier, I had joked with him that I was a little bit of a neat freak.

When I walked into The Accountant's house, I breathed a huge sigh of relief. His tidy house had classy, modern furniture and décor. Mature trees and bushes covered his outside patio and backyard, and he had a fish pond. He was a grownup living in a grownup house. No handcuffs hung on the headboard or barbells in the living room.

The Accountant and I went out with each other at least once a week, whenever we were free. I stopped counting how many dates we went on when we hit the double-digit mark. Happy that I could have an intelligent conversation with him, I was glad that he didn't get caught up in any drama. He appreciated my intelligence and humor and he made an effort to read my previous books.

The Accountant showed off his excellent culinary skills to me many times and always brought something to my house when I cooked. He grew fresh vegetables in a garden, like me, and had a good handle on his finances. (Of course, he did. He was an accountant!) Plus, he always immediately kissed me every time he saw me and never showed any jealousy of my male friends. I couldn't believe that someone like him existed. Oddly, The Accountant and I primarily corresponded over text. I counted on one hand the times we chatted on the phone.

When we went to a party at his friend's house, I quickly met new people. The Accountant and his friends talked about a Jimmy Buffet concert three months away. In front of them, he turned to me and said, "Oh, you don't know about this. Do you want to go?" I think I stood there speechless for a few moments but eventually said yes. I hoped this was a good sign that he wanted me to stick around for a while.

A couple of weeks later, we attended another friend's party. We arrived incredibly late because I had a prior commitment, so I felt bad and brought some made-from-scratch chocolate pudding (one of my favorite recipes). We mingled with The Accountant's friends for an hour before he pulled me aside and suggested that we get the pudding for everyone. While I got the pudding and whipped cream out of the fridge, I laughed as I watched him pillage our host's cabinets for individual serving dishes and spoons. Grateful that he helped me dish out the pudding, he didn't expect me to do everything. He surprised me as I learned more and more about him.

Later that month, I suggested to The Accountant that we go to Paint Night, where a local artist walks everyone through how to paint a selected acrylic piece. I had painted most of my life, but I assumed this left-handed, left-brained accountant would never be interested. To my delight, he said it sounded like fun. He had never painted before and was a trouper. I quickly realized he did this for my benefit. Another plus.

By the third month, The Accountant and I texted every day (still no phone talk), had weekly dates, and shared our daily life events. One Saturday morning, he wrote a flirty text to me that said, "I am writing out my To-Do list for the weekend and you are at the top."

We still hadn't divulged our feelings for each other, but I liked him. For the first time in a long time, I was genuinely enamored. He didn't disclose his feelings for me, but his actions spoke volumes. Regardless, my friends told me countless times that they assumed he was smitten with me, too. While on vacation for a week with his daughters, he vented his frustration that we couldn't get together as often as he liked. I told him we could talk about it when he got back.

When The Accountant returned home, I suggested a couple of ideas for us. I first told him that we'd have to make a conscious effort to see each other on the weeks that I had my kids. Up until then, we never had a set date night.

Then, I offered that he could meet my kids. He took a deep breath and told me that he didn't meet kids unless he thought a relationship was serious. We had only been exclusively dating three months, but I didn't refer to him as my boyfriend.

Caught off-guard with his statement that he didn't think we were serious yet, I figured I could give him a few more months to see if he then felt differently. If we reached six months and he still didn't think we were significant, as much as it pained me, I would have to move on. In the meantime, I wanted to keep moving forward and he seemed to agree. I assured him things would be better after I took my kids on vacation.

The following week, I took my kids to Florida. While on vacation, The Accountant was hit or miss with his texts with me and went a few days without any contact. His unusual behavior surprised me since we had always texted every day. I hoped he was simply giving me space so that I could enjoy my vacation.

When I got back, we had been apart for two weeks and I looked forward to seeing him. I sent The Accountant a text asking if he wanted to go hear a local blues musician the following night. He said it sounded like fun, but had other plans with friends who came into town - and, for the first time, he didn't invite me to come along. I had plans to go visit my sister over the weekend, so I wondered if The Accountant understood that he wouldn't see me for several more days.

I took matters into my own hands that night and stopped by The Accountant's house, unannounced. Never having done that before, I couldn't predict his reaction. He invited me in, we sat on his couch and caught up, since we hadn't seen each other for so long.

Then he said to me, "You know how we talked about our relationship a few weeks ago?" I looked at him with wide eyes. He said, "I don't think we should date each other anymore." I stared at him for a few long moments, trying to process everything. I finally spoke and said, "I had a gut feeling when you were out of touch while I was on vacation."

He went on to say that he didn't foresee things getting serious between us and that we were in two different places in our lives; I had kids at home and he didn't. I guess our age difference factored in after all. I took a deep breath and said, "Would you tell me if I hadn't stopped by tonight?" He said yes, but I found it difficult to believe him. I started crying. Not buckets full, but enough to show my distress.

That awful, emotional night bore down on me. Earlier that night, The Professor showed up after eight months away. (Worst. Night. Ever.) I told The Accountant that I liked him and, for the first time, he said he liked me too. Through tears, I said, "But I don't want to be with someone who doesn't adore me." I stood up from his couch and gathered my keys. The Accountant leaned in and hugged me for a long time. And then he quickly kissed me on the mouth. He hugged me again. When he kissed me on the mouth a second time, I broke the hug. He sent me mixed signals for someone who had just broken up with me.

When I left, I immediately called Denise in tears. She reassured me that it wasn't me and that The Accountant had commitment issues. I wanted to believe her, but my fresh wounds prevented me.

The next day at work, I lamented to one of my co-workers about what happened. He said, "Does this guy know what he is walking away from?" I guessed not.

Three weeks later, I had lunch with my friend Christi at a local deli. The Accountant walked in with a coworker, stopped, and chatted with us for a few minutes. I hadn't seen him since the night he broke up with me. Christi told me that he sat two tables behind me and faced us. (Maybe he did this so he could watch me as he ate his lunch?) He didn't make it awkward, but my heart jumped a few extra beats. Happy that I wore a short skirt and killer heels, I wanted him to see what he missed.

Lesson #13: Nice, normal guys do exist even though they might not be for you.

Chapter 14

Gray Areas

How do you know when you are in an exclusive relationship? What are the defining factors? What is the timeframe? I would think that a handful of dates does not constitute exclusivity. But if I am seeing someone frequently for more than two months, the thoughts of a monogamous relationship surely run through my mind. However, I might not be ready to call him my boyfriend. "Boyfriend" is a high-school label, but once the term is used, it clears up a lot of relationship status questions.

Seeing someone exclusively doesn't have to include the boyfriend title. Does he think the same thing about me? Finding out if he has gone out with someone else would be a jab to my heart (and ego) after we have spent all that time together.

But I hate flat-out asking someone if I am the only person that they are dating. I don't want to sound needy or like I'm looking to define the relationship. And if sex is on the table, I can't imagine finding out that the guy that I am dating is seeing someone else. Nor would I put someone else in that position. Another reason to wait for sex. What's a girl to do?

While I dated The Accountant, friends of his encountered this grey area. This event unlocked the topic for me and I told him that I wasn't dating anyone else. He said the story of his friends wasn't his intent to get me to open up, but I still wanted him to understand my intentions. Then I said to him, "I told you that I wasn't seeing anyone else. Are you?" I took a deep breath and waited for his answer. He said no and that was that.

I get that every conversation is not that simple, but I opened the line of discussion about me first. I did not put The Accountant on the spot and I think he appreciated that.

My friend Catharene once suggested a 90-day review for me. I had been seeing someone for a few months, wondering if we were exclusive, and I was nervous to talk to him about it. Catharene told me to treat it like a job review and say to him, "It's been 90 days since we've been seeing each other. How am I doing?" The topic turns onto me and my companion can exhale.

But if I am casually dating multiple people, I want to do the right thing and be upfront about it. And sex is a no-no if many people are involved. Once sex is on the table, the whole game changes and is not fair to the other people who aren't having it.

How do I tell someone that I am seeing someone else as well? I am not sure since I haven't been in that situation.

Lesson #14: If you want to know if you are in an exclusive relationship with someone, talk to them about it.

Chapter 15

Serendipity

One late Sunday afternoon, I returned a movie to my library. The place was closed for the day with one lonely car parked in the lot, but no one was in the driver's seat. As I walked up to the library's front porch to drop my movie into the after-hours box, a man sat on the stone wall of the porch, working on his laptop. He looked to be a few years younger than me and had a hipster beard.

"You do know the library is closed?" I said to him, probably startling him.

"Yes, I know," he replied and looked at me for a few seconds.

"Oh, so then you're waiting for someone?" I asked.

"No, doing some work," he said, still looking at me.

"You're using the free Wi-Fi?" I asked, more of a statement than a question.

He chuckled and said, "Yes, but it's also quiet here."

I didn't want to bug him, so I let him do his work. The window of opportunity for me to talk to someone opened widely and I went with it. Nothing else happened with the guy at the library, but that doesn't mean something couldn't happen in a similar situation with someone else. I am not letting these opportunities slip away because I am too shy to talk to someone.

Kelly had a comparable experience. One morning, she stopped at a local convenience store on her way to work to get some coffee. A man in line clearly checked her out. She purposely stood close enough to him to get a better look at him and to make sure he didn't have a ring on his left hand. He dressed in a suit for work but had a skull on his keychain. Kelly liked the idea that he could have a bad-boy streak in him. Intrigued, but Kelly couldn't find a way to break the ice with him and the opportunity slipped away. Maybe she should have dropped her coffee on the floor? Then he would have had a reason to help her and talk to her.

Another night, I was out getting drinks with Michele. She kept glancing at a hot guy at the other end of the bar. I urged her to go over and talk to him, but she was chicken. A few minutes later, he walked past us. Tapping him on the shoulder, I asked him a question. I introduced him to Michele and they chatted for a few minutes. When he left, she turned to me and said, "How did you just do that?"

I said, "All you have to do is ask."

Lesson #15: Every moment can be an opportunity to meet someone.

Chapter 16

Breaking Up is Hard to Do

I like to think that I am not a heartless bitch. I'll try my best to be kind when I have to break up with someone. If a man isn't worth a second date, I hope that I can be upfront and mature enough to tell them that I am not interested in pursuing things any further. I'll try hard not to disappear on someone either. The man might be hurt hearing my explanation at the moment. But in the long run, I think it will be best for everyone.

I've heard various ways in which people break up. For all those guys who aren't man enough to end things and decide to disappear instead, I say, "Shame on you." Why do you do that? Because you don't want to break the girl's heart and watch her cry? Come on. I get that people break up all the time and things don't work out. Look at the numbers. People break up more often than they stay together. You'd think we would get better at it and finally learn how to do it right. But since that's not always the case, I've come up with a list of things not to say when breaking up with someone:

1. Don't call me "amazing" when you are breaking up with me. I don't like to be patronized. If I am so amazing, then why are you ending things with me? Save that for a girl who has zero self-confidence. I don't want to hear it.

2. "We don't have chemistry." How is that possible? We must have had chemistry at one point. Otherwise, you wouldn't have asked me out for a second date. And a third. And a fourth...

3. "I don't think we should see each other anymore." Ouch. This is upfront and to the point, but it's still hard to hear. I can't force you to want to be with me. (Maybe this is the best thing to say?) But when you tell me that, you should have a legitimate reason for ending things. If you don't see a future with me, then tell me. I am a big girl. I can take it.

4. "I love you, but I am not in love with you." This phrase always confused me. These two phrases should go hand-in-hand. Don't bother telling me you love me to begin with if you aren't in love with me. Maybe he should have said he liked me, not love, and it was too late to take it back?

5. "Let's be friends." You're joking, right? I have never slept with my friends. Maybe in a year or two when I am not so angry at you for breaking up with me, maybe, just maybe, we can be friends. But right now, you can forget it. I have enough male friends.

6. When it's time to break up, be an adult and do it in person. If that isn't possible because it's a long-distance relationship, call the person and do it over the phone. Never, ever break up with a text message, unless the person is violent or crazy. I cried a little when The Accountant broke up with me, but he didn't freak out because

a few tears scared him. He sat still and let me cry as I tried to process everything. He was an adult and did it in person.

7. Don't disappear. Even though it's a trite expression, give the person some kind of closure. That word is so overused, but it's true. When someone disappears, no matter how much I want to know what happened, I refuse to be the crazy stalker girl who shows up demanding answers. As hard as it is not to understand, sometimes it's best to walk away from the situation. Months later, when I have moved on, I will be proud of myself for being a mature adult.

8. When you break up with someone, give them the space to move on. Do not check in on them every day for the next two weeks to ask how they are doing. That only keeps the wounds fresh. They need time to heal and to get on with their lives. They aren't mourning the loss of the person who broke up with them, but all of the possibilities the relationship offered. When Michele's boyfriend broke up with her, he continually called her and texted her all hours of the day and night. She found it hard to move on. I ran into him a week later and flat out told him to give her some space and to leave her alone. It was out of line for me to say that to him, but I cared about her. I wanted her to be happy again and he prevented that from happening. Two months later, he still contacted her almost daily. We attended a mutual friend's party and he came up to me and said, about Michele, "You know I still love her." I think he wanted me to take his side, but I didn't take the bait. I told him that I did not trust him because he had hurt Michele. He needed to get his life in order before he had even the slightest chance to get back with her. If she would even let him.

When a guy breaks up with you, don't call him a few weeks later to ask how he is doing. Just don't. Think about it this way - If you ended things, would you want him calling you?

Lesson #16: When you break up with someone, be mature and be honest. Make every effort to do it in person at their place.

Chapter 17

The CPA

A few weeks after The Accountant broke up with me, I had plans to go to a college alumni event. My friend Mike would be there and I looked forward to catching up with him since I hadn't seen him in six months. The day before the event, Mike sent me an email that said, "I am not looking to send you into the fire so shortly after The Accountant, but do you remember The CPA?" (Apparently, the word on the street was that I was an accountant groupie.) I knew of The CPA in college. We had mutual friends, but I couldn't remember if our paths ever crossed. Mike told me The CPA had plans to be at the alumni event the next night and Mike wanted to reintroduce me to him.

The next night, even though I arrived five minutes late, I was the first guest to walk into the restaurant hosting the event. The event coordinator was the only other person there, so I chatted with him for a few minutes, briefly discussing the attendee list. We stood at the back of the restaurant at the bottom of the steps leading up to the second floor, where our event was being held. Me, being the short person that I am, stood on the bottom step so that I could view the entrance to the restaurant. I think I stopped mid-sentence when a tall, handsome man wearing a cut suit walked in. I couldn't remember the last time someone looked that good in a suit. As the man in the suit walked toward us, I said to the event coordinator, "That looks like The CPA." (Keep in mind, I hadn't seen The CPA in almost 20 years.)

The CPA and I exchanged pleasantries for a couple of minutes, but we weren't sure how to break the ice with each other. I couldn't say to him, "Oh, Mike wanted us to hook up..." Fortunately, Mike walked in a few minutes later and helped us feel more at ease as the three of us got a table on the second floor. As we talked over beers, The CPA disclosed his prior marriage but had no kids. He didn't sound bitter at all when he explained that his ex-wife left him for someone else. When I told the guys about my misadventures in online dating and how I attracted 40 possible suitors in a week, The CPA said, "Why wouldn't you? You're a catch." I blushed 16 shades of red and sheepishly thanked him.

An hour and a half later, The CPA told us that he had to leave because he had a prior commitment. As he stood, I told him (in front of Mike) that I didn't have a business card on me. The CPA promptly reached in his pocket and handed me his. After The CPA left, Mike asked about my plan. I told him I didn't play the three-day waiting game, so I would either email The CPA the next day, which was a Friday, or wait until Monday. Mike agreed that either would work.

The next day, I waited until 3:30 p.m. to email The CPA because I didn't want to seem too anxious. Among other things, I told him it had been good to catch up with him and that I hoped to hear from him soon. He emailed me back on Monday morning and immediately suggested that we get drinks and dinner. But as we compared schedules, we realized it could be a couple of weeks before we could get together. I had my kids for the week and he had plans to go out of town the following week. In no rush, I could wait. We emailed each other every day but kept things casual as we learned more about each other.

The day after I ran into The Accountant at the deli, I emailed Mike and told him what happened. He said, "I suppose you'll have to be aware of inter-firm rivalry among the CPAs in the area. If you wind up on a date with The CPA and bump into The Accountant, you may be the cause of a full-on gang-style fight between their firms, worse than the Crypts and the Bloods. You may want to bring a weapon." I barked in laughter as I read it.

As I gradually told friends about The CPA, they wanted to see what he looked like. To my good fortune, several online articles featured him - with pictures! All of my friends declared him hot. We found a picture of him riding his motocross bike and he personified a total badass. I was glad he wasn't an uptight suit married to his job. When I told Mike what my friends thought, he said "For the record, I, too, think The CPA is hot. He would beat me out if there was a

People's Sexiest CPA Alive contest. He is the Bradley Cooper of bean counters."

A week later, The CPA and I finally met for drinks. He had come straight from work still dressed in a shirt and tie. He sat at the bar with a glass of red wine waiting for me and immediately hugged me when I walked up to him. We talked for an hour and never experienced an awkward silence. He asked me about my kids, my dog, and my work. I learned about his family, the seven marathons he had run in the past 20 years, and his snowmobiling adventures. He showed me a picture of himself on the snow and I said, "You are quite the badass." He laughed out loud. When he told me he had plans to go out of town the following week for work, we realized it would be a couple of weeks before we could get together again. Regardless, the date went well.

The CPA and I chatted every few days over the next month, but we couldn't secure a second date. Our schedules clashed. He didn't seem to want to make much of an effort and I gave up trying. He is still a nice guy. That being said, he knew where to find me. I wasn't about to chase him.

Lesson #17: If someone doesn't make an effort to see you, then they aren't interested in you. Simple as that.

Chapter 18

The Dating Bucket List

Everything you need to accomplish before finding The One:

1. Spend Thanksgiving dinner alone.

I didn't spend Thanksgiving alone, but I did spend Christmas Eve alone.

2. Learn to live with yourself.

I have a house and a dog, and don't mind spending nights eating dinner on my couch watching bad TV. I can admit that I am a little OCD and can be a little snooty about things. I'm perfectly content watching movies by myself and taking day trips on my own.

3. Take time off between dating people exclusively.

Get your shit together and allow yourself to heal. Some people jump from marriage to marriage, not figuring out who they are and never learning to live by themselves. I knew a woman who left her husband in January, the divorce finalized in April, she met someone else the following week, and was engaged again by November. In my opinion, it was too quick. If you take time off, the next person will appreciate that you've taken some time off to learn about yourself.

4. Date a coworker.

Before I made the decision not to date co-workers, I tried it. The co-worker and I went on a few dates and kept it a secret amongst our fellow workers. That brief relationship didn't work out for other reasons, but he and I still say hello when we run into each other. People sometimes meet their spouses at work and others who have had ugly experiences. Either way, dating a coworker might be something to try.

5. Cut your hair.

Chopping your hair has nothing to do with dating, but the metaphor is to make a change in your life. Besides, it's *only* hair.

6. Take some road trips with friends or, better yet, by yourself.

The solo trip I took to Arizona to visit The Professor was the best thing I could have done for myself. The liberating trip allowed me the freedom to only think about myself. I hadn't traveled on my own like that since college.

7. Date a neighbor.

All of my neighbors are either retired or married. I'm out of luck with that.

8. Make sure anyone you're dating can admit that they are over their ex.

Even if they don't mean it, the first step in getting over an ex is saying it out loud. Besides, you don't want to be with someone who is still hung up on someone else. The same goes for you. Even if you have been broken up with someone for a while, if they are still in your head, you aren't over them yet.

9. Allow your heart to be crushed.
Everybody needs a good heartbreak. Who wants to go through life without one of those in the emotional scrapbook?

10.   Forgive.
This is where you grow up. Let go of the anger and the hurt. You don't have to forget what happened, but forgiving is a good step.

11.   Join a Meetup group.
Do something for yourself where you will meet new people. After I left my ex-husband, I joined a salsa dance group. I met a lot of great people, men and women.

12.   Date someone at least 10 years older than you.
If the person is in good shape and can keep up with you, I say go for it.

13.   Date someone at least 10 years younger than you.
Who said women can't have a young stud on their arm? Several men flirted with me who were at least 10 years younger than me. I went out with one of them and we had fun.

14.   Have a one night stand and slink away.
Three words - use a condom. (And if he comes to your place, don't let him sleepover.)

15.   Kiss a stranger, and then walk away.
This will take a lot of liquid courage to pull off, but can you imagine being on the receiving end of that? (I doubt men could get away with this, but I wonder if most women could?)

16.   Speed dating.

Could be an interesting experience. I'll document it if I ever do it.

17.   Go to a bar by yourself.

Nervous that all of the other bar-goers would stare at me, it wasn't as bad as I assumed it would be. The pub had a few local entertainment rags for me to read while I sipped my gin and tonic, so I didn't have to sit staring blankly into space.

Lesson #18: Make a dating bucket list for yourself.

Chapter 19

Online Dating Part Deux

Eventually, I felt better about the whole concept of online dating and decided to try it again with Plenty of Fish. What was the harm? If I didn't like the outcome, I could always choose to not meet anyone and deactivate my account again. One Friday night, while down and out with a head cold, I decided to create a new online profile for myself.

Once again, I warned those who communicated to me with only a "Hi" or a "Hey" that they shouldn't expect a response. I asked open-ended questions. Within the first 36 hours, 35 different men contacted me. Only five of them wrote "Hi" or "Hey" and were immediately deleted. They obviously didn't read my profile and only looked at my pictures. Other grounds for elimination included living over an hour away, having only a high school education, and having the relationship status of "separated." Some women I know eliminate guys who are fans of an opposing football team or have too many cats. I liked to think I was more open-minded.

Several of the men who responded to my profile were of a different ethnicity than me and I didn't care. One of them bluntly said that other women he encountered didn't care for his "shade of tan" (yes, that's what he said) and he hoped that I was different. Was he serious? I couldn't believe the intolerance of these other women. I reassured him that skin color does not make the man.

A dozen of them were 10-15 years older than me. Maybe they were smart, interesting men, but I wasn't interested in someone that much older than me or being someone's arm candy. I replied to them saying that I was honestly looking for someone closer to my age and wished them luck on their search. One older guy replied and said, "How do you know unless you try?" I didn't respond and deleted the message. Then he messaged me again the next day and said "Well?" Are you kidding me? His desperation clearly showed and I deleted the message again. If he had sent me another message, I would have had to block him.

Another 55-year-old contacted me and, when I read his message, something seemed off. His sentences skipped words, wrong words were used, and contained several grammatical errors. Maybe he was scamming me? Then he asked the question, "How do you feel when you achieve one of your goals?" He read my bio but gave a lackluster attempt at my request for an open-ended question.

I replied saying that I was genuinely looking for someone closer to my age, skipped his bizarre question, and wished him luck in his search. He replied with this (yes, it's verbatim with the punctuation errors, because I couldn't do it justice paraphrasing): "Thanks ...no problems at all . I am looking for a women that mature enough to stay with me, so she may inherit all my assets after my death during a massive orgasm :) Good luck dear." My mouth fell open as I read it. I joked with Kelly that I missed out on being his trophy wife and rich widow.

After a week, men continued to contact me. But this time I didn't freak out and was happy to find that I had learned from my previous online experience. I still wasn't sure how to maintain a conversation with a total stranger without coming off with canned questions like, "What are your hobbies?" Maybe play "Two Truths and A Lie" to let the real talk begin?

I had given my first name to several of the guys and still felt safe. A handful of the men said they wanted to meet me, but I thought about logistics. I had my kids every other week, so those evenings were out. But I could have lunch with the guys if they worked near me. And I had to work around their work and kid schedules too. Would it be terrible of me to have lunch with one man and then drinks with another guy that same night?

I bought myself a small notebook to take some notes on each man. I wanted to remember who was who and keep track of names, ages, occupations, information about their kids, and even if they drank socially or were a teetotaler. The notebook seemed overkill to write everything down, but it seemed almost impossible to keep all these guys straight without taking annotations.

A few men stood out from the rest, but I still found it a little overwhelming, trying to figure out how to narrow them down. Not a slave to the site this time, I made my own rule to only be on it once a day. I stated in my bio not to be discouraged if I took a few days to respond while letting the men come to me. After all, a lot of men like the chase, right?

Other avenues existed to meet men, so I treated the online experience for exactly what it was: an introduction arena. Fate was in my hands. And if I didn't like what I read online, I could always walk away. I didn't owe anyone anything on the site, not even my first name.

After a few weeks, I got at least one new message from someone each day in addition to the men with whom I was already corresponding. I realized I didn't have to respond to everyone every day, nor did I have the time for it. Some men had to wait a few days to hear back from me. I think my approach showed my interest but didn't bleed needy.

The site sent me a notification every time someone said they "want to meet me." I must've received 50 of those notices and deleted them. If the guy could not be bothered to send me a real message, I didn't want to meet him.

Several of the guys gave me their phone number, asking me if I wanted to talk to them outside of the site. Hesitant to do that, because, once I called them, they would have MY phone number and I wasn't ready for that. I still didn't learn exactly who these people were, so I didn't want to give out any personal information yet. But one man in particular said to me "... if you are comfortable with it, I can give you my number, and we can talk outside the site." I told him I wasn't ready for that and he was fine with it, but I appreciated that he asked. Showed good character. (But then he didn't contact me again.)

Another man insisted on having my phone number. I tried to be nice at first, telling him I don't give out my phone number until I meet someone. He wasn't deterred. He said he needed it in case we met somewhere and he was delayed and needed to reach me. We weren't even to the point of setting up a date, so he jumped ahead of himself. Again, I told him I didn't give out my phone number to total strangers and wished him luck. He replied and said, "...glad to see you are already raising your red flag and I can avoid you." Wow, what a jerk. I tried to be safe and he acted like I was in the wrong.

I told Allan about the imbecile and he responded in an email: "[This guy] is a scared pup. He thinks you had a special connection and he is hurt that you are dating other people (which is weird because you didn't even tell him that and, in fact, you are legitimately busy over the next couple of weeks). He thinks you SHOULD feel the same way and be prepared to clear your schedule. What you see here is not a man. It is a boy. Any 'man' who sends messages like that to a girl before a first date has some serious emotional issues they need to reconcile. If I were him, and you sent me a message like that explaining your schedule, the proper response, whether you are interested or not, is 'Sure sounds good! Let's touch base when things aren't so busy and see where we are at.'

"It gives both parties the option of backing out and, most importantly, it is RESPECTFUL. He will be on your dating website when you are deeply into your next long-term relationship. Pushing for your number, even though you made it clear what your boundaries are, was hardly a classy move either. Is it this difficult for guys to figure out how to date? Any man who approaches this with a sense that you owe him something will not succeed with you or any other woman." Admittedly, Allan sounded preachy and self-righteous but he had my best intentions at heart.

Finally ready to meet some of these men, I wanted to be incredibly safe. When I set up a date, I sent several of my friends photos of the men I planned to meet, texted them when I arrived at the location, and texted my friends again when I left.

I even had Paul come with me on one date. He stayed far enough away so the guy I met didn't notice him, but Paul still had me within eyesight the entire time. Horror stories of women getting assaulted on dates still scared the crap out of me. Being overly safe is never wrong when it comes to meeting a stranger.

Nervous about what to talk about on these first dates, I went to Allan for advice. He gave me some inside information and said the surefire way NOT to get a second date is to talk too much about myself. He directed me to make sure the conversation is two-way: Ask my date questions and ask him questions about the answers he gives me. According to Allan, there is a Guys' Rule of 10. Allan said if a guy asks me 10 questions before I have asked him one, then I have failed the Rule of 10 and I will not be asked out on a second date. He also gave me a few edgy questions to ask:

- If I were to ask for references from your exes, what would they say?
- What did you want to grow up to be when you were a kid?
- What kind of things are you passionate about?

I took those questions and went a little further to learn what these guys "believe in." You know... the "I believe..." speech that Kevin Costner gives in Bull Durham (one of my favorite baseball movies). The speech goes something like this: "I believe in the soul, the cock, the pussy, the small of a woman's back, the hanging curve ball, high fiber, good scotch, that the novels of Susan Sontag are self-indulgent, overrated crap. I believe Lee Harvey Oswald acted alone. I believe there ought to be a constitutional amendment outlawing Astroturf and the designated hitter. I believe in the sweet spot, soft-core pornography, opening your presents Christmas morning rather than Christmas Eve and I believe in long, slow, deep, soft, wet kisses that last three days..." That speech is decades old but takes my breath away every time I watch it.

Here's my speech: I believe in good whiskey, honesty, faithfulness, flirting, and having the car door opened for me. I believe in exchanging small gifts on Valentine's Day and the power of a good kiss. I believe in raising respectful kids, keeping a clean home, and making omelets on Saturday mornings. I believe in putting my phone away, traveling to new places, and reading a good book. I believe that the third date does not automatically equal sex. I believe in balancing a checkbook and paying my bills in full and on time. I believe in keeping napkins in my car because I am bound to spill something on myself. I believe in calling when you are late, dressing nicely, keeping promises, and having good manners. I believe in laughing at myself and finding out how big of a buffoon I can be sometimes. I believe in dancing at weddings, sending Christmas cards, hosting parties, and laughing out loud. I believe in spending time with the people I care about. I believe in good hygiene, good grammar, patience, and not sweating the small stuff. I believe in learning how to change a tire and saving room for dessert. And... I believe in love.

Lesson #19: Online dating is a good introductory arena.

Chapter 20

Interviewing

I finally decided to meet some of the men I was talking to online. I giggled every time I told someone that I had three dates in one week and two more the following week. Who has dates with five different men in 10 days? Two of those dates happened the same day - lunch with one and drinks that night with another. I didn't tell any of the men that I planned on meeting the others, because I didn't owe any of them explanations this early. Nor did I want to put pressure on the men that they competed with other men for my attention.

* * * * *

Bachelor #1 and I met for lunch. He told me he was 100% Greek and his olive complexion confirmed it. He had impeccable manners, so his Greek momma taught him well. He left me to get a napkin to clean the crumbs from our table, he picked up our orders, and he took all of our trash away at the end of lunch. He seemed nice and a good conversationalist, but I wasn't feeling anything. As hard as I might try, I couldn't force a spark. Later that night, he emailed me through the site and asked if I wanted to go out again. In an email the next day, I thanked him for lunch and told him that it was good to meet him. I declined a second date with him because I didn't think that I was the one for him. Hopefully, he appreciated my candor and that I didn't lead him on or waste his time.

* * * * *

Later that night, I met Bachelor #2, whom I'll call The Great Dane Guy, at the local dog park, where Paul watched from a distance to ensure my safety. The Great Dane Guy was accompanied by his Great Dane, who weighed more than I did. The Great Dane Guy and I talked about our respective dogs and our kids. The sun started to set after 45 minutes as an indication for us to head out. The Great Dane Guy asked me if I wanted to go out again. He seemed interesting enough. I said yes, but I told him I had a rule that I needed to learn someone's last name (so that I could run a background check to make sure he doesn't have any assault or stalking charges against him... or worse) before I went out on a second date with them. He chuckled and told me what his last name was, but I didn't have a pen on me to write it down. He understood the requirement for the second date, so the ball was in his court. Almost a week went by before he emailed me his last name, but his background check came back clean. I decided I wanted to see him again.

* * * * *

Two days later, I met Bachelor #3 for a drink. Like Bachelor #1, this guy was nice enough, but nice doesn't equal chemistry. We sat at the bar and talked for about an hour. After a few awkward minutes of silence, I quickly commented about the baseball playoff game on the TV in front of us. I wondered if he was thankful that I filled the silence with man talk. He volunteered his last name to me a few times, so I didn't have to come out and ask for it. After an hour, he asked if I wanted to do it again. To break the awkward feeling, I joked that I needed to run a background check on him first even though I didn't want to see him again. I texted my friend Kristin when I got home and told her it went "okay." She said, "I figured as much since you are home so early." I didn't hear from Bachelor #3 again, but I didn't care. I had others in the lineup.

After those first three dates, I figured out a benchmark to qualify it as a good date: Do I want to kiss the guy? Kissing someone is intimate and personal. I have to have some basic level of attraction to someone to want to kiss them. If I don't feel some kind of attraction to the guy on the first date, I probably never will, and I shouldn't waste his time or mine by going on a second date with him. I pondered that romantic relationships could develop from friendships, but I didn't want to kiss any of these first three bachelors. The Great Dane Guy was the closest, but my hesitancy reared its ugly head.

* * * * *

The following Monday I met Bachelor #4 for lunch. The website stated his age as 45. He told me his two daughters were 21 and 9. As I did the math in my head, he said, "... I got married in my

30s and then we had our first daughter." Come again? If he was 45 and his daughter was 21 and he got married late, the math didn't add up. I asked him, "Well, how old are you?" He said 55. Then he explained that his buddies had filled out the site profile for him and he couldn't change his age. I questioned his validity and wondered what else he hid from me. Seemed fishy to me. Next.

Before I dismissed him, Bachelor #4 asked me if I had encountered any crazies from the site. I could honestly tell him I hadn't. Nor had anyone misrepresented themselves with a 20-year-old picture. Normal, regular guys. Apparently, this was a rare thing from what I heard from other folks. At this point, I was more overwhelmed with the quantity of men than the quality. I ran my stats from the site and 75 men had contacted me in less than a month. Most of them were quickly weeded out because they failed to read my profile, but even half of that was hard to corral. I was selective in who I wanted to meet so far. Less than 10%, at this point. Three hundred men viewed my profile in less than a month. 300! I flattered, but part of me was glad that they all didn't send me a message because I felt it was impossible that I could have kept up.

* * * * *

The next day, I met Bachelor #5 for lunch. He flat out asked me how I made out on the dating site. I told him I had several dates already with more planned. I had nothing to hide. He had a choice if he wanted to continue contact with me discovering that he had competition.

He asked me what my intentions were and I chuckled a little bit and compared it to interviewing for a job. I was, after all, looking for the best candidate for me. I assumed he was deterred, but he said he wanted to go out with me again. The following day, I looked at my calendar, compared my kid schedule and his, and realized we didn't have a free night until three weeks later. I told him about the night being so far in advance but he wasn't deterred. Honestly, if someone told me they weren't free for three more weeks, I might not wait that long. Something always comes up.

I found Bachelor #5 boring and didn't want to waste my time or his. I later found out from a coworker who knew Bachelor #5 that he was demeaning to women, a "keep 'em barefoot and pregnant" type of guy. I dodged a bullet because he and I would have had words about that. He would have learned quickly that I don't stand for sexism.

After five mostly lackluster dates, I discovered a guy needed to be worthy of a second date with me. I would not assume each guy was Mr. Right and then set myself up for disappointment when he wasn't. I told myself to have fun meeting each one and let myself be pleasantly surprised if I did find someone worth dating exclusively.

* * * * *

The following week, I met Bachelor #6, whom I'll call The Happy-Fun Guy, for lunch. He looked better than his photos and was the cutest man I'd met so far. I wasn't sure what to expect because he didn't have a college degree, but his sense of humor made up for it. Unlike some of my other dates, he made me laugh. As we walked out of the restaurant, he held the door for a few elderly ladies and the one said to me, about him, "Is he available for sale?" I said,

"Not today... but he is cute, isn't he?" He stood alongside me, so he definitely heard me say it.

Even though The Happy-Fun Guy was only five years older than me, I found out the following week that he had an infant grandson. I'd never had to think about dating someone with grandchildren, so this was a first. But I opened my mind and wanted to go out with him again.

* * * * *

Bachelor #7 gets a dedicated chapter...

* * * * *

I had connected with Bachelor #8 on the first go-round of online dating and he found me again. Hesitant to go out with him because he was eight years my junior, I finally decided to give him a chance. We met for dinner at a local, noisy pub, but we had a lot of fun talking, laughing, and poking fun at each other. The date went a lot better than I had expected. I didn't envision myself in a serious relationship with Bachelor #8, even though he and I could still be friends.

* * * * *

Bachelor #9 reminded me a lot of The Great Dane Guy. He was decent-looking and seemed to have a good handle on his life. He teased me that I didn't have a smartphone at the time, and called me Pocahontas, because, without a smartphone at the time, I'd need to send out smoke signals to communicate with someone. When Bachelor #9 and I said goodbye after our lunch date, I asked him what his last name was. He stated it, and I responded, "Get out..." He asked, "Why? What?" as if I meant he was related to the

President. I told him I had the same common last name. We quickly surmised that all of his relatives were local and mine were not, so it was practically impossible that we were related. I'm sure he panicked for a moment. I did. Nevertheless, I laughed. I found out a few days later through Kristin's husband that Bachelor #9 was a notorious "hothead and a douchebag." After already being married to someone like that, I was not about to do it again. Pass.

* * * * *

I met Bachelor #10 out for lunch the following week. He was attractive and dressed well, but he barely spoke. Bachelor #10 didn't volunteer anything about himself unless I asked. I needed to be with someone who gives more than minimal short answers when I ask him questions. Was this guy nervous or introverted? I struggled because I don't want to carry the conversation with anyone. At the end of lunch, I was surprised that Bachelor #10 asked me for a second date. I told him my rule of getting a last name before I agreed to a second date. But he didn't tell me at that moment though. Bachelor #10 never got back to me with his last name, so I didn't have to worry about telling him that I was not the one for him.

* * * * *

I found that Bachelor #11 talked as much as I do, which is a hard thing to do. However, he talked a little too much about his ex-wife. He didn't sound bitter at all, but he violated an unspoken rule for a first date. He just met me and told me intimate details about his former life. This conversation bordered on awkward for me, but I tried to keep an open mind. A few days later, he sent me a message asking me for a second date. I told him my rule about getting a last name and he turned it around and asked the same of me. Smart man.

I didn't eliminate Bachelor #11 at this point.

Lesson #20:   Determine benchmarks for why you want a second date with someone.

Chapter 21

The First Date that Almost Wasn't

I had plans to meet Bachelor #7 one evening at a coffee shop two miles from my house. I arrived a few minutes early and stood outside on the sidewalk to wait for him. Five minutes went by. Okay, I thought, he must be running late. I sauntered down the shopping center sidewalk and spent a few minutes eyeing the yummy cakes in the nearby bakery window. Upon returning to the coffee shop, still no Bachelor #7. Half a dozen people came in and out of the coffee shop. None of them fit his description. Ten minutes went by. Seriously?! Miffed thinking that I was being stood up on our first date, I decided to give him five more minutes. Five more people went in and out. Bachelor #7 did not have my phone number, so he couldn't get a hold of me if he was running late. After 15 minutes of waiting, I said the hell with him and left.

When I got home, I logged onto the site and read a message from Bachelor #7 five minutes before we planned to meet. He claimed his car wouldn't start and he was waiting for his daughter to come home, so he could take her car. He asked me not to leave. I sent him a quick message, saying that I had been to the coffee shop, and left. I also told him that I lived five minutes away, and I would go back to the coffee shop to meet him.

When I finally met Bachelor #7 at the coffee shop, he said he was happy that I came back. I immediately said, "This is what I get for not having a smartphone." (I got one a month later.) He said he realized he didn't have my phone number to call me and had called the coffee shop, giving my description. The barista told him that no one matched my description. I'd been outside on the sidewalk and the barista hadn't seen me.

Bachelor #7 hadn't completely blown me off and conscientiously tried to get a hold of me when he was late. One point for him. But things didn't work out with Bachelor #7. He only talked about himself and didn't ask anything about me. He wasn't rude or arrogant but didn't seem to be interested. Honestly, I was a little bored. I guess Allan's Rule of 10 works for women too. This is Dating 101...

Lesson #21: Good guys try to reach you when they are running late for a date.

Chapter 22

Kicked out of the Stable

One night, I was supposed to have a date. The operative words are "supposed to." The guy never showed up. He texted me 30 minutes ahead of time, saying that he was on his way. I texted him back confirming it, but he never showed.

I like to give people the benefit of the doubt, but at some point, shouldn't common courtesy come into play? If something came up (his grandmother needed a ride to Zumba class, his pet fish wanted an underwater bicycle, he couldn't decide on which paper towels to buy...), I don't care what... he should have had the decency to send me a text saying he couldn't make it. I get that things happen and cause delays (I am guilty of it myself), but I don't like being stood up. Who does?

We had had other dates, so this wasn't our first date. And, by the way, this was the THIRD time he stood me up. Shame on me for giving him more chances.

The first time, I called him out on it and he profusely apologized. Apparently, he fell asleep. The second time, he proactively apologized without me saying anything. And this third time... nothing. He sent me a quick hello text a few days later and didn't even mention missing our date. I deleted the text without responding. A few days after that, he sent me another quick text. I replied saying that I was mad at him. He said he figured as much. I reprimanded him for his lack of common courtesy. All he had to do was send me a text saying something had come up and tell me that he wouldn't make it. He didn't reply.

I kicked him out of the stable.

Lesson #22: Bad behavior and lack of common courtesy come with a price.

Chapter 23

Second Dates

I went on a second date with The Great Dane Guy two weeks after our first date. We met at 9 p.m. at a local pub. Over a couple of beers, we sat at the bar, watched baseball, and talked. I sat a little bit closer to him, brushed his arm with my hand, and knocked his knees against mine, hoping he took notice of my moves. We laughed and talked, and I never felt any awkward silences. At one point, I looked over at the clock on the wall that read 11:30. Two and a half hours had gone by and I hadn't even noticed.

He held my attention, but the late hour prevented me from staying longer. I grumbled that I had to get up the next morning for work. When The Great Dane Guy walked me to my car, he immediately hugged me and kissed me on the cheek. He said he had a great time. He lingered a few minutes at my car, then leaned in and quickly kissed me on the mouth a few times. His kisses were an unexpected sweet surprise. We talked about going on a third date and I told him that I wanted to go out for dinner next time. He agreed. I said goodnight and drove away.

Over the next two weeks, The Great Dane Guy kept in contact with me. He texted me roughly every day, but he didn't suffocate me. Sometimes he initiated the first text and sometimes I would, but he ALWAYS got back to me. I never felt like he was ever blowing me off, even though he spent a lot of time coaching his sons' sports teams and, of course, working.

One night, Michele and I were out to dinner and I playfully texted The Great Dane Guy that I had had too much wine. He immediately offered to come pick me up, so that I wouldn't drive. Michele and I ended up staying at the restaurant for three hours and, by the time I left, I was sober enough to drive. Nevertheless, I was impressed that The Great Dane Guy looked out for me.

After the second week, we finally went out on our third date. I told The Great Dane Guy that I wanted to go somewhere that I could wear something other than jeans. I wore a short white, backless dress with a short black moto jacket. We ate at a Spanish tapas place and shared several plates. (BTW, the food was excellent!) After the waitress cleared our dishes, I leaned forward and rested my hands on the table. The Great Dane Guy reached out and, cutely, held my hands in his. As we walked out, he placed his hand on the small of my back and then held my hand as we strode down the sidewalk. This guy understood how to treat a woman on a date.

Throughout the night, The Great Dane Guy told me several times that he loved what I wore. My short jacket didn't completely cover the open back of my dress. I asked him if he saw the low back of my dress underneath my jacket and he said no. We walked over to a pub across the street to watch the seventh game of the World Series and sat at the bar. He had his hand on my back again and I said, "Give me your hand" and put his hand right below the back of my jacket, so he could touch my bare skin. He smiled wide at me.

Despite his protests, I picked up the tab for our beer. We stayed at the pub for an hour and then he drove me home.

When we arrived at my house, I told The Great Dane Guy he could come inside for a little bit to watch more of the game. Once inside my house, we stepped into my kitchen and he wanted to see the back of my dress. I took off my jacket, turned around, and showed him my backless dress. He said he liked it. I cautioned him and told him that the backless dress was not coming off; he agreed. Then he really kissed me. And kissed me again. And again. This man knew how to kiss.

At 10:30 p.m., he reluctantly said he should head home. Happy that he brought it up, I didn't feel like a jerk kicking him out of my house. I didn't want him to hang around my house wondering if something else materialized, only to find out I wouldn't sleep with him.

The Great Dane Guy was a gentleman and told me he wanted to go out with me again. He seemed to be a good mix of awesome, manly, and gentle, all at the same time.

Lesson #23: Let him wine and dine you.

Chapter 24

Moving On

Right around Halloween, I found out that The Accountant started seeing someone new. Finding that out hurt. Part of me hoped he was happy; part of me wished that the new woman looked like a dowdy librarian. But regarding him and his discriminating taste of the women he dates, the woman was fantastic. I hoped to avoid running into him with this new girlfriend, even though I had been out on many dates since he broke up with me.

Later that same day that I found out about The Accountant's new love, I ran into Kevin who had introduced us and I told him what I learned. At that moment, I had a revelation. I told Kevin that I needed to be with someone who wasn't afraid to be around my kids and The Accountant wasn't that person. (Nor was The Professor, for that matter.) My kids aren't needy babies, but they are a huge part of my life and I usually cannot spontaneously plan things, because I have to work around their schedules. That's how it is. I'm not wasting my time with someone who won't meet my kids. I deserve better than that and so do they.

I am commitment-shy these days because I am afraid of falling too hard and too fast, and getting hurt again. But at least I understand what I am looking for. Maybe this was the non-verbal vibe that I gave off to the recently superfluous men in my life?

A month later, I met another man 10 years older than me who had sons in their 20s. Let's call him Jay Gatsby because of his exorbitant wealth: three homes, five cars, including a '69 Camaro SS, a plane, and six racehorses. According to Denise, who introduced us, he "had so much money he didn't know what to do with it all."

Jay Gatsby humbly didn't flaunt his massive wealth when I met him for drinks. He seemed like a genuinely nice guy, but I was concerned about the age difference and that I had kids at home and he didn't. Jay Gatsby could spontaneously fly off in his plane to go to his house in Florida. I couldn't, because I had priorities with my kids. I presumed that if he wasn't willing to be with someone who had priorities like that, then he wasn't the one for me. Nor did I want him to later resent me for not being available for him. I worried for nothing because he didn't ask me out again. Jay Gatsby eventually found a woman who complemented his lifestyle and later married her.

This got me thinking. I was pissed that The Accountant refused to meet my kids and broke up with me because of it. Shame on him for passing up a great catch because of his rule. I didn't ask to marry him. I simply wanted him to be part of my life. Obviously, he was wrong for me.

Lesson #24:   If someone isn't a good match for you, that doesn't mean they can't be a good match for someone else.

Chapter 25

Laws of Attraction

Michele met a guy at a Halloween party and he dressed as an Army Airborne Ranger, complete with a maroon beret. He had a good build and a chiseled face. After talking to him for a good hour, she confided in me that she would go out with him if he asked her. She said he seemed nice and didn't set off any initial red flags. As I walked past him, I leaned into him and said, "You need to give Michele your number before the end of the night." (It's always good karma to be a valuable Wingwoman.) An hour later, he handed Michele his business card. Score one for Michele.

The next day, Michele looked the guy up on Facebook. They shared some mutual friends, so she easily found him. After seeing some of his pictures, her giddiness took a nosedive. The guy looked like Steve Carrell in *Dinner for Schmucks*, with half as much hair. She felt terrible for being so shallow, but she couldn't get past the fact that he had little hair. The choice of the beret as part of his costume made perfect sense. She confessed her attraction to guys with hair. She didn't end up calling him after all. At least she was honest with herself in admitting what she likes and what she doesn't like.

I think everyone has personal standards for what they find attractive in someone else. Some guys like tiny women. Some women like tall men. I want a man who is at least four inches taller than me. What can I say, I like to wear heels and I don't want to tower over the guy. In addition, I like fitter guys. When a guy is healthy, I can presume he cares about himself and isn't lazy. He doesn't have to be a gym rat (hell, I'm not), but, if he's fit, he at least grasps that exercise is good for him and doesn't shrug it off.

But what if the man is fit, and his wife used to be hot and has let herself go? I've seen it happen many times. Did he look past some things early in the relationship when he was distracted by her outside appearance? Or is he a foolish, shallow prick who needs to be physically attracted to his wife because her appearance won't be enough, no matter how great she is on the inside? Is he wracked with guilt because he should be attracted to her physically and he is ... not? Or is he a petty shithead who only wants a hot wife?

Conversely, what if a still-attractive woman married a man with a full head of hair and six-pack abs and, years later, he has neither? Do both people expect an implicit bargain that both parties try to remain within the same parameters? Maybe the unspoken deal shouldn't matter, but it does and most people can't run from it.

Lesson #25: Know and admit what you find attractive.

Chapter 26

Toughest Critics

The Great Dane Guy met three of my best girlfriends one night for our fourth date. When I asked him to come out with us, I said, "How do you feel about hanging out with four beautiful women?" He said, "How do I feel?... I feel like a king with a harem!" I was glad that he wasn't intimidated at all.

The five of us met at a local restaurant for appetizers and drinks. Niki and Michele sat on one side of the table and The Great Dane Guy, Kelly, and I sat on the other side. Kelly sat on the end, diagonal from the group since no one sat directly across from her. Seeing this, The Great Dane Guy leaned into me and whispered, "I feel bad for your friend. I should have sat over there, so she doesn't have to sit on the end." I was glad that he was cognizant of someone else's feelings and made an effort several times to draw her into the conversation.

Throughout the night, my girlfriends asked The Great Dane Guy a lot of questions about himself and watched if he took offense to anything they said. He didn't. I watched for his reaction and silently wondered if my friends did the same thing. He took everything in stride and laughed with us. He didn't say anything out of line and asked my friends questions about themselves, too. Throughout the night, he held his hand along my lower back and I occasionally rested my hand on his thigh. The only joke that The Great Dane Guy didn't get was when Kelly said, "My gynecologist told me about this restaurant...." and we girls lost it. He didn't understand the humor and I had to explain it to him.

After talking for almost two hours, we all decided to call it a night. When the four of us girls reached for our wallets to pay for our drinks, The Great Dane Guy informed us that he was picking up the entire tab. My girlfriends and I sat dumbfounded for a moment. We'd intended to pay for ourselves and had never expected for him to do that. But The Great Dane Guy insisted and we thanked him immensely. Kelly later told me that she watched The Great Dane Guy talk to the waiter on the sly, guessing that he intended to foot the whole bill.

On our way out, The Great Dane Guy kissed me in front of my girlfriends. He said he enjoyed meeting them and had a great time. All three of my girlfriends told me later that they liked The Great Dane Guy. They would tell me if they didn't like him because they want me to be with someone who treats me and others nicely. He did that. They didn't want me to be with a know-it-all or someone who couldn't keep up with four energetic women. They have seen me with crappy men who have complained about me yawning in front of them (ahem...The Professor), and they don't want me to make the same mistakes again. I was glad that he got their seal of approval.

Lesson #26: As a litmus test, have your best friends meet your new guy and watch how he responds to them.

Chapter 27

Phasing Out

After two months, I decided to take down my online dating profile. My mom planned to visit for a month and I wouldn't have time to go out with anyone. I couldn't say, "Hey mom, I'm leaving you alone, so that I can go out on a date." That would never go over with my mom.

I tallied up the stats: 11 dates, 110 men sent me a message, 220 wanted to meet me, and 440 checked out my profile. If I say so myself, 10% was selective. If I wanted, I could have met so many more. The pool seemed endless. If anyone ever asked me if I had a good experience with online dating, I would have to say yes. I didn't run into any creeps or players. My filter system worked against anyone who sent me a canned message that would be sent to any woman regardless of what her profile said. Some of the men I encountered were genuine and sincerely looked for their Ms. Right. Before I deactivated my account, I sent a message to those guys (i.e.

Bachelor #11) and wished them luck without disappearing. I hope they appreciated my gesture. If I wanted to reactivate the account at a later time, I could.

On the day before I deleted the account, I received an odd message. The simple message read: "Hey, how are you? I am from [your town] too." I normally would have deleted a fleeting message like that, but the man it came from aroused my suspicions. The photo looked much like one of my old coworkers, someone who had left two years earlier. We had been friends when we worked together but lost touch once he resigned. He and I had never dated though because I found him too neurotic. Here's the kicker: That former co-worker got married two years earlier and I ran into him and his wife a year later.

I replied to his message and said, "[His first name], is that you?" I didn't know his marriage situation, even though his relationship status on the site said single. I wondered if he was stepping out on his wife. He didn't reply but instead removed his photos from the site. The next day, the account was deactivated. Seemed fishy to me. I would bet anyone $100 that he was still married. Even though I barely knew his wife, I felt bad for her. Goes to show that some men on these sites have no problem cheating on their wives.

Lesson #27: Be selective with who you meet.

Chapter 28

Good Words vs. No Words

The Great Dane Guy asked me to go with him to get his son's Christmas present on a Saturday afternoon. The day before, he sent me a sweet text saying, "Hello, my Saturday shopping love…" Wow! He had called me "honey" a couple of times before, but this was the first time that he used the word "love" when talking to me. I never heard him call anyone else that as a throw-around word, so I hoped he was selective with it. When I read that text, I couldn't stop smiling for a good hour. Happy that he was comfortable enough saying it to me, I wasn't anxious.

We had only known each other for six weeks, so everything was still new and early for us. The fact that he used that word even as a nickname showed that he planned to go somewhere with me. People in general, mostly guys, tend to shy away from using the word "love" in any form during casual dating. I do. These words are not something to even joke about. I don't want anyone to freak out too soon in a relationship. Especially if I am the one freaking out.

New territory for me, I couldn't remember the last time a guy said anything like that first. Twenty years ago when my ex-husband said it to me when we dated. Not The Professor, not The Volleyball Player, not The Accountant. To be fair, once I said it to The Professor (eight months after we reconnected), he continually told me he loved me, even after I broke up with him. My point: I was the one who said it first.

I didn't even get an "I like you" from The Volleyball Player or The Accountant. I don't hide my emotions, so I did tell both The Volleyball Player and The Accountant that I liked them. Neither of them said anything back to me and left me in awkward silence. Two swings and misses for me. I didn't want to get called out on strikes, so I kept my mouth shut lately.

When The Great Dane Guy called me his love, he was different. He knew how he felt and he wasn't afraid to tell me. I wasn't some arm candy, filling a void for him.

I think everyone likes to hear how someone else feels about them. We all have scars from previous relationships, and we expect more scars from our new relationships. When someone can't even tell you that they like you back, it's defeating and a sign of rejection.

After all, you weren't asking to hear the word love. Love is reserved for deep commitments and the time when you're ready to introduce the kids. But, like... that's for someone who has gotten past a third date and has made his way to second base, maybe even third. That giddiness makes you smile when you think you fantasize about a future with this person. Where would you live? Would you spend your weekends at a football game or at a farmer's market? What do you get him for Christmas?

You don't say any of those things out loud, because you don't want to freak out the person, so you simply tell them you like them. And you wait, with bated breath, and hope that they say it back to you.

Lesson #28: A man should tell you early on how he feels about you.

Chapter 29

Is it serious?

After two months of casually dating The Great Dane Guy, we had yet to say if we were in an exclusive relationship. I had taken down my online dating profile but wondered if he had taken his down. Then opportunity knocked.

Michele decided to take the plunge and signed up for the same dating site that I had used. Fresh meat and overwhelmed with emails from men on the site, she asked me to help her weed through. I logged on as Michele and searched for The Great Dane Guy. I smiled when I couldn't find his profile. If he still had an account, my giddiness would have dropped like a lead balloon. I checked twice to make sure. This was a good sign.

The following week, my parents visited me for Thanksgiving. My mom is a seamstress and had made my dog a winter vest for the previous year's polar vortex. I volunteered her to make a vest for The Great Dane Guy's Great Dane. She agreed but had one caveat. My mom needed to measure his dog. Great Danes are not average-sized dogs. That meant The Great Dane Guy would need to bring his dog over to meet my parents. I nervously asked him to do so thinking of how The Professor refused to spend time with my family, but my hesitation was unwarranted. The Great Dane Guy immediately agreed. He worried about what to wear, but I told him we dressed in casual jeans and t-shirts. My mom measured his dog and then we sat with my parents for an hour and chatted. My mom later told me that he seemed nice and easygoing.

Ten days later, I was scheduled for some low-risk surgery. The Great Dane Guy voluntarily took off work to get me discharged from the hospital and get me situated at home. He made sure I had everything I needed and showed me compassion and caring that I hadn't seen in a long time. Earlier, The Great Dane Guy had offered to stay overnight with me in the hospital to make sure I would be okay, but his schedule didn't allow that to happen. Was he for real?

Two weeks after my surgery, I itched to get out of the house because I was going stir-crazy. The Great Dane Guy took me ice skating, holding my hand the entire time. He had played hockey for a junior team of the NHL and I had been skating since I was five, so we were both fine on the ice. After skating, I struggled to bend over to untie my skates, because of my abdominal surgery. He promptly lifted my legs on top of his knee and untied my skates for me. sweet.

While we sat there, I told him it was new territory for me to date someone who had kids around my kids' ages and was unsure of the best time to bring them into the mix. He told me it was completely up to me when we did that. I wasn't sure how or when I would, but he didn't run away from the idea of meeting my kids as several others had before him.

The next night, The Great Dane Guy came over for dinner. My mom had made her homemade meatballs before she left, so that was the main fare. After we ate, The Great Dane Guy gathered up the dinner dishes and started washing them in my kitchen sink. I told him he didn't have to do that and he said, "I wash dishes at my place, so why wouldn't I do them here?" That blew me away. No one had ever washed my dishes before.

The next few weeks were hectic for both of us with the holidays, the flu bug going around, inclement weather, and kids' events. His kid-free weekends didn't match up with mine, but we still tried to go out with each other as often as we could. Unfortunately, The Great Dane Guy and I got together for a total of an hour over those weeks and I got frustrated that I couldn't see him more. He must have picked up on my vexation (or had some of his own?) because he voluntarily left his three teenage sons for two and a half hours on a Saturday afternoon to spend time with me. I was tickled!

The Great Dane Guy and I still hadn't had any kind of serious talk about our relationship, but we had been casually dating for four months reaching my threshold. I wanted him to meet my kids because I craved spending more time with him.

Lesson #29: Actions speak volumes.

Chapter 30

Worst Date Ever

Michele had, what she called, the Worst Date Ever. She met the man online and, despite my objection and personal rule, gave him her phone number before they met. He texted her several times a day supporting her gut feeling that he would be clingy. They finally decided to meet two weeks later.

The man lived over an hour away from Michele and he volunteered to come to her town to get together. She wasn't keen on him being right in her backyard, so Michele suggested a restaurant halfway between them. He agreed.

While they ate, he reached across the table, grabbed Michele's hand, and insisted that living an hour away from each other could work. The man then told her the story about an ex-girlfriend of his who lived several states away. (And I swear this next part is true.) He wove the tale of how he deeply cared for his ex, but their sex life was not what he had hoped. The man described in detail the first time he and his ex attempted to have sex. The woman immediately cried, creating a major buzzkill. He later found out she cried because her lady parts were too small to accommodate him. Aghast, Michele couldn't believe what she heard. Who tells someone on their first date how large their penis is? Topics on first dates usually include hobbies, kids, and work, not the size of a man's penis.

Michele politely listened as her date finished the story. He expressed that the subsequent sex with this woman was less than stellar. Michele felt terrible for the woman; this man went around telling someone he just met about his ex's lackluster sex skills. Even though Michele couldn't wait to leave and had no intention of seeing this guy again, she endured the rest of the meal without arousing the suspicion that she had an abysmal date.

The next day, the man texted Michele five times in five hours, asking her how her morning went, and told her he'd had a great time with her. She and I went out to lunch that day and she showed me his fifth message, the one that pushed her over the edge. He wrote, "What are your thoughts on our date? On us? On our future?"

I could usually give sound advice, but I simply had no words for her. They had one date. How could he possibly ask Michele her opinion of their future together? This guy had bigger cojones than she thought. Michele had a gut feeling she couldn't let this guy down easy and had to be straightforward with him, even if it meant hurting his feelings. A few hours later, she texted him back explaining no future between them. He replied and said he sensed the same. Certain that she had bruised his ego, Michele concurred he agreed only to save face. She was thankful she didn't hear from him again.

Compared to Michele's date, my dates seemed normal. No one was rude, offensive, or arrogant. Boring? Yes. But not arrogant. I was lucky.

The worst date I ever had happened when I was 17, but still topping the bad date list for me. I worked at a restaurant at the time and the young dishwasher continually asked me out. I finally said yes because I didn't see the harm in it. When he came to my house, his friend sat in the car and was going on the date with us. What? Who brings a friend on a first date? I didn't complain about it but thought it was a little strange. My date took us to an all-you-can-eat buffet restaurant and I ended up paying for both of us because he didn't bring any money. Who asks a girl out and expects her to pay on the first date? His buddy had empty pockets as well, but I refused to pay for him. His friend sat with us while we ate and, at one point, grabbed a fork and started eating off my date's plate.

A few minutes later, the restaurant manager came by and told us that we were not allowed to share food and, if he witnessed it again, we would have to leave. Great, now we risked being thrown out of a restaurant. Could this date possibly get any worse?

My date and I finished eating, we left the restaurant, and we all went to his house to hang out. I was nervous that his parents weren't around. While we talked, his phone rang and he snatched it up. I could only hear his side of the conversation, but he said, "Yes, I am here. I have to take Mary home, but I'll be back after that." After he hung up, I asked him if his parents called. He said, "No, my probation officer. I have to check in with him every night."

Kill. Me. Now.

Lesson #30: Laugh about your worst date.

Chapter 31

A kiss is just a kiss... or is it?

I'm a big fan of kissing: a peck on the cheek, a graze on the mouth, or full-on tongue. I think of it as a sign of affection. Kissing can happen practically anywhere at any time. (Well, maybe not at work.)

I ended up going on three dates with The Happy-Fun Guy. We had a great time on our second date and spent four hours together. The date culminated at a local coffee shop that closed at 10 p.m. and I could tell that The Happy-Fun Guy didn't want to say goodnight yet. He lingered a little at my car but made no indication that he intended to kiss me. I took the initiative, leaned in, hugged him, and kissed him on the cheek. Still nothing. Maybe my single-girl-sense lost its power and he didn't like me as much as I inferred?

The Happy-Fun Guy was hit or miss. Some days he texted me all day, but then I wouldn't hear from him for a week. He was a good guy, but I could never guess where I stood with him and assumed we were not exclusive. I continued to date The Great Dane Guy (who DID kiss me on the second date).

Six weeks after I met The Happy-Fun Guy, Michele and I went out to dinner. We talked about some of the guys she had been talking to online and one of them was The Happy-Fun Guy. I didn't mind the potential of her going out with him, because I never had anything serious with him. If he wasn't the right fit for me, then I hoped he could be a good fit for her.

She told me that they had chatted a few times, but then he disappeared from the site. Not a fan of someone disappearing, I decided to call him out on it. I texted him and asked him why his profile was gone. He sent me a quick text back, saying he didn't purposely disappear. Regardless, he didn't remember Michele. I told her what he said and she said, "Oh, I bet I never gave him my real first name." That didn't deter me from thinking that maybe I should introduce them soon.

Fifteen minutes later, The Happy-Fun Guy called me and wondered why I asked him about his online dating presence. He overheard the background noise of the restaurant and asked me if I was out on a date. I hesitated, chuckled, and said, "No, I am out with Michele." He accused me of playing him, but I assured him otherwise. I told him that I had no problem with him going out with Michele. I hung up and ordered another drink with Michele.

A half-hour later, The Happy-Fun Guy texted me and asked if Michele and I were still out. I told him yes and invited him to join us. He showed up 20 minutes later and got a drink with us. We all laughed, compared online dating horror stories, and had a no-holds-barred conversation about the unwritten rule of two girls going out with the same guy. I still had no problem with Michele going out with The Happy-Fun Guy and felt no jealousy at all. Along the same lines, The Happy-Fun Guy told me that I went out with one of his buddies... Bachelor #7. We had all crossed lines and had a minimal degree of separation.

A half-hour later, we decided to call it a night. When we said our goodbyes, I hugged The Happy-Fun Guy. He still did not attempt to kiss me. I figured he wasn't interested; we could still be friends. He seemed like a good guy, after all. Or maybe since I gave him the green light with Michele, he was more interested in her?

The next morning, The Happy-Fun Guy called me. When I insisted to him again that I didn't care if he asked Michele out, he hesitated. He finally said, "I am not interested in Michele. Why do you think I am calling you?" I knew he had some kind of interest in me, but his signals blurred so I didn't assume he liked me. I said to him, "I had no idea. Yes, I thought we had a good second date, but you didn't even attempt to kiss me that night." He listened while I spoke again. I said, "If a guy likes a girl, he usually kisses her to show it."

I have no problem speaking my mind, but I shouldn't have to tell a guy to kiss me. He should do it. The Happy-Fun Guy then asked me what I had planned for the day. My daughter's basketball game was scheduled for early afternoon. When he asked if we could get together afterward for a late lunch, I said yes.

I met The Happy-Fun Guy at a local bar mid-afternoon. He immediately and oddly kissed me as he stepped closer to me. His mouth was closed and the kiss was dry as if no one had ever shown him the benefits of kissing. I had wetter kisses from my grandmother! We sat, ate lunch, and talked for an hour.

When we were done, we got up and The Happy-Fun Guy leaned in and kissed me again. I cringed at the same dry, lifeless kiss. After the first kiss, I had hoped I imagined that it was bad, but the second kiss proved my suspicions. I hope he hadn't noticed my frown.

I debated if I could go on another date with The Happy-Fun Guy, remembering his poor kissing skills. But I didn't have it in me. Someone might think that's shallow of me to dump a guy because of his lackluster kissing abilities. But if I am dating someone, I want to be able to kiss him any time I want and it won't be good for me if the guy is a bad kisser.

Lesson #31: A good kiss can set the pace for so many other things.

Chapter 32

I know better

What could I have been thinking? I shouldn't have even pondered it once, much less twice. No, I didn't do anything wrong, but I shamefully have to admit my temptation. I could rationalize that these things happen to the best of us, but I wouldn't even believe it. Nor am I a self-righteous bitch who thinks she has no flaws. Let me explain.

A couple of weeks before Thanksgiving, I shopped for a new car. I had done my homework and knew exactly what I wanted, down to the color, so I didn't waste any time running from dealership to dealership. My current car had a recall on it, so I took it to be fixed. At the dealership, I met The Car Salesman and test drove the car that I wanted with the intent to buy by the end of the year. The Car Salesman was personable with me. He asked me lots of questions about myself and told me some things about himself. My guard was on hiatus because I couldn't even tell if he was flirting with me or desperate to sell me a car.

While I drove, The Car Salesman told me about his stint in a local rock band. Then I noticed the wedding ring on his left hand. (I must have been distracted by the shiny new car because we single girls are quick to look for that.) Okay, so he was married. I grasped the concept of staying away from him, but my single-girl-sense still gave me an indication of his interest in me. Before I left The Car Salesman that day, I told him I would contact him next month when I wanted to purchase the car.

The following month, I emailed The Car Salesman, ready to buy. I bet he jumped out of his seat when he got that email as it was probably the easiest sale he had all year. A few days later, I sat in front of him to sign the initial paperwork and to pay my deposit. I asked him if I could get the car delivered in time for Christmas because I wanted to tell my daughter that Santa brought it for me. He said he would do his best. He again was personable with me, but not outright flirting with me. I usually sensed when a guy flirts with me but my barometer bounced all over the place.

Three days before Christmas, The Car Salesman called me and told me my car had arrived from the other dealership. I hoped that my daughter might still believe in Santa if a car magically appeared in front of the house on Christmas morning. She had been wavering for the last couple of years.

However, being the only driver in my house and not trading in my current car, I wasn't sure how to drive my old car to the dealership and then drive both cars home. The Car Salesman quickly volunteered to come pick me up from my house. Nervous that he would find out where I lived, I hoped he did it because it was part of his job. But I agreed.

Once we arrived at the dealership, he showed me my new car with all its bells and whistles. The Car Salesman affably told me several times to call him if I had any problems with the car and gave me his cell number. When I asked him to open the hood of the car, so that I could check out the engine, he said, "Don't you have a man in your life to do these things for you?" I chuckled and said, "You're funny!" Maybe I should have asked him if he had a woman at home whose hood he could open? He again said for me to call him any time that I had problems. I left a little while later with my brand-new car.

A few days after Christmas, my daughter popped a string on her guitar. I am uninformed about guitar strings and didn't have a clue where to get it repaired. Remembering The Car Salesman being in a band, I emailed him asking if he could tell me where to go to fix it. He recommended buying a new string at a specific music shop and then he would repair it for me for free. He then offered to come to my house and replace it for me. I wasn't comfortable with that at all and countered that I would bring the guitar and the string to the dealership.

On a Monday, a week later, I brought the new string and the guitar to the dealership. The place was a madhouse. People ran around everywhere. Car dealerships are usually never this busy. The Car Salesman spent 10 minutes with me to replace the guitar string and then he scurried off. His demeanor came off as professional, not personable like the first time we met. When I left, I comprehended that he had not been flirting with me at all and my confusion lived in my head. He had obviously only wanted to sell me a car. No harm, no foul.

Later that night, while out to dinner with a couple of girlfriends, my phone rang. I stepped away from the table to take the call. The Car Salesman called me to apologize. He restated the craziness at the dealership earlier and expressed regret for not spending much time with me. He told me about his upcoming gig with his band that coming Saturday and invited me to come watch.

When I sat back down with my girlfriends, I wondered what to think. If he had been simply looking to sell me a car, would he have called to apologize for not spending more time with me? If I platonically went to watch his band play, would that lend itself to inappropriate opportunities?

On the fence, I told my girlfriends what was going on. I didn't mind being in a public place with him, but at the same time, I didn't want him to think we could go somewhere private. Never clarifying the situation with him, I wracked my brain with all sorts of possibilities.

I didn't want to be that girl who his wife called in a jealous rage, saying "why are you talking to my husband?" That wasn't who I was. I don't break up marriages. I would have nothing but good intentions if I went to listen to his band play. I didn't need some insecure wife finding out that I was at the bar and confronting me, or him.

Life's a whole lot simpler and fun when you don't tempt fate or stir up jealousy. The only thing that threw me off the right path was had he been single, I would have gone out with him. The lines blurred. Choosing the right option is safer when the other person is not someone I would be interested in. I can easily say no to someone who is not appealing to me.

A couple of days later, I took my new car out in the snow and stopped at the library a mile from my house. I parked and my driver's side door would not open from the inside. I could unlock and lock it, but it wouldn't open. I called The Car Salesman in a panic. He had told me several times to call him if I had any issues with my new car, so I took him up on his offer.

I told him what happened and asked if he was aware of this in other cars like mine. He said no, but suggested that I open the passenger door from the inside, then go out and around and open my driver's side door from the outside. His suggestion worked.

The Car Salesman then said, "I am not even close by to help you, honey." Whoops. I think he caught himself calling me 'honey.' I heard the catch in his voice, but I didn't say anything. He again asked me if I planned to watch his band play that Saturday. I said I wasn't sure. I wanted to go hear his band, but I ultimately decided not to. Avoiding trouble, I stayed away from a married man.

A couple of months later, I took my car to the dealership for an issue and The Car Salesman chatted with me for a good 20 minutes. When he walked me out, he lingered at my car for a few minutes and hugged me goodbye. I had a hunch he didn't hug all of his clients like that.

Nine months after I bought my car, my cell phone rang with a number that looked familiar to me and the man on the other line said, "Hey beautiful, how are you?" Umm.... Who is this? Then he said, "It's been nine months since you bought your car and I was just calling to see how it's running for you." Maybe most car salespeople are instructed to follow up with their clients, but I doubt many of them call their clients "honey" or "beautiful." I think if I gave him the green light to go out, he would jump all over it, but I stayed away.

Lesson #32: Even the best of us are tempted.

Chapter 33

No excuses

Three days after Valentine's Day, I gave up on The Great Dane Guy. I didn't expect red roses or a Coach purse, but a card and maybe some chocolates would have been nice. Something. Something to show me that he cared about me. My teenage son even grasped the concept that he needed to buy something for his girlfriend on Valentine's Day. The Great Dane Guy didn't get me anything for Valentine's Day. Not even a cheesy card. I was hurt.

Valentine's Day was a test for me. Back at Christmas, I bought The Great Dane Guy a soup crock with a logo of his favorite football team and made him some scratch-made Maryland crab soup. (The soup was delicious if I do say so myself.) I gave it to him four days before Christmas, thinking it was plenty of time for him to still get me something.

Due to circumstances beyond our control, we didn't get together again until a few days after New Year's. He didn't have anything for me. Isn't it common courtesy when someone buys you a Christmas present (especially when you are dating them) to reciprocate and get something for them? I was incredibly upset and disappointed. Neither The Professor nor my ex-husband gave me anything for our first Christmases together, so this was a sensitive issue for me. (Plus, The Professor completely forgot my birthday one year.) I didn't want to ignore the red flags again.

Six weeks later, when Valentine's Day rolled around, I decided not to get The Great Dane Guy anything. I hoped that he would make up for not getting me anything at Christmas. Nope. Nothing.

I quickly realized where I ranked on his list of priorities. I didn't understand it. Why did he volunteer to take off work to drive me home from the hospital when I had surgery two months earlier if he didn't plan to get me a Valentine's Day gift?

Everyone I told this story to scratched their heads as well. They witnessed how well he had treated me up until Christmas.

But my patience expired. If he couldn't make an effort to think about me on Valentine's Day, I shuddered to think about what he wouldn't do when my birthday rolled around a few months later. My birthday was the one day of the year when everything should be about me. I didn't want to stick around and find out.

I did everything right with The Great Dane Guy. I didn't rush in and fall hard and fast. I dated other people in the beginning, trying to figure out the best man for me, and I liked The Great Dane Guy the most. He impressed me in so many ways early on and I was genuinely happy around him. I was comfortable around him too, more so than anyone else in a long time. I found the balance between coming on too strong and showing too little interest. He told me some personal things about himself and his family. He let me in. We had a lot in common and had the same attitude about life -- not to take it too seriously, because something always came along. But, apparently doing the right things didn't work.

I told Allan about the lack of a Valentine's Day present and he wrote this in an email: "My advice is that the punishment should fit the crime. Your response should have a degree of equality to his level of effort (or, lack thereof). I would put your profile back up on your dating site. Start dating again and not say a word about it to him. You owe him nothing. This is CHEAP AND LAZY. There are NO excuses. And remember this – I WAS THE GUY STANDING UP FOR HIM AT CHRISTMAS. Now, even I am done.

"Regardless of what you feel about this guy, he is NOT meeting your needs. You are NOT compatible. You deserve to be with someone who sees eye-to-eye with you on this and shares the same values and common sense. You cannot FORCE common sense or values. Another point to ponder: If this is how your first Valentine's Day with this guy was, can you imagine how lame it would be in 2, 3, 5 years? I'd be surprised if he remembered your name.

You guys just started dating. This was HIS TIME to impress you. If EVER there was a time to dress nice, talk nice, be nice, and do your best, it was now during the audition. HE FAILED THE AUDITION. There may be other parts out there he is better suited for, but that is not your concern. Your leading man is still waiting to be cast. Seriously, if he was here right now, I would tell him THANK YOU and GO F*CK YOURSELF. The "thank you" would be for keeping the bar so low. It makes it easier for the rest of us to look good. Suddenly my Coach purse is worthy of a f*cking statue... of my penis."

Even though Allan's response was over the top, he was right. The Great Dane Guy did not meet my needs. I wanted more but I am not needy. I don't feel it's necessary to text someone all day, every day, asking him where he is or what he is doing. But I still have needs.

I wasn't hanging on to be hurt because he didn't get me anything for Christmas or Valentine's Day. I would eventually resent him for it. As much as it pained me to end the relationship, I deserved better. The Great Dane Guy had no excuse to not get me a Valentine's Day present.

Lesson #33: If a man isn't meeting your needs, it's best to move on, no matter how you feel about him.

Chapter 34

The Magic Formula

I am throwing this next chapter over to my friend Holly. She is a life blogger and cancer survivor. She wrote this piece on pinkfortitude.com. Take it away, Holly.

Are you dating Mr. Maybe or Mr. Right? How do you know the difference between Mr. Right Now and Mr. Forever? How do you know that your man is The One? Today I will share three examples from my life and then offer up the magic formula.

When I was single, I always said that I would rather be alone than with someone who wasn't right for me. When Carter and I met, I was completely jaded and blew him off. I even broke up with him two months after we started dating. His pursuit finally wore me down and I decided to get serious with him. Little did I know how much our lives would be turned upside down. Little did I know that the worst year of our lives would give us the magic formula and transform our relationship to where it is today.

Love Example #1

Let's begin with the sweetest love story of all time. My parents. My dad knew in the second grade that he would marry my mother. They have now been in each other's lives for 60 years, married for almost 50 of those years. When my mother was 25 years old, she found out she was pregnant with me. She also found out that she has Addison's disease, a "severe or total deficiency of the hormones made in the adrenal cortex, caused by its destruction." She has had years where it's been in remission and years where she is in and out of the hospital frequently. My dad has stood by her all of those years, and loves her more every day.

Love Example #2

I was diagnosed with breast cancer on my 39th birthday. Carter proposed 48 hours later. We got married 10 days after my treatment ended. I was sick and bald on our wedding day. To say that our engagement year was hijacked is an understatement. It was one of the worst years of our lives. But looking back, it was the best year of our life together. We learned about unconditional love and support. We learned how to love each other during the most difficult of times. From that point on, everything is relative. A normal married couple fight? It's got nothing on cancer.

Love Example #3

The other week, I said goodbye to a childhood friend. My friend Garnet was diagnosed with brain cancer at the same time as I was diagnosed with breast cancer. He fought hard for four years before losing his courageous battle. He is survived by his wife Trish, and two young boys, ages five and one. Trish's life was turned upside down, not only having to take care of two children but also a terminal husband. Her poise and grace during those four years were inconceivable.

You know those marriage vows? The one that is about "in sickness and in health?" That is the magic formula. It's easy to be in love. It's easy to forget about life around you and be so engrossed in your significant other that nothing else matters. It's easy to think that this euphoria will last forever. Maybe you are one of the lucky ones. But life isn't always rainbows and puppy kisses. Sickness happens. Cancer happens. Ask yourself, "If this man was sick or diagnosed with cancer, or terminal, would I stand by him unconditionally?" More importantly, ask yourself, "If I was sick or diagnosed with cancer, or terminal, would he stand by me unconditionally?"

Don't think it can't happen to you. No one can predict the future. Take a hard and honest look at your relationship. Is he the man who will endure? Don't live in your fantasy world and don't think he will change. He's either in it or he's not. And if he's not, walk away. Open your heart to the one who will stand by you through sickness and in health. He's the one who is worth waiting for. He is the one you deserve.

What about you? How is your dating situation? Or on the flip side, what is/was your determining factor to know when he is Mr. Right?

Love, hugs, and I do, for better or worse.

Lesson #34: True love is being there for someone. No matter what.

Chapter 35

Armchair therapy

The movie *The Perks of Being a Wallflower* has a great quote in it. Emma Watson's character Sam asks, "Why do I and everyone I love pick people who treat us like we're nothing?" Her friend Charlie replies, "We accept the love we think we deserve." Let's repeat that. We accept the love we think we deserve. Why do we think we deserve so little?

We are all amazing people and we should be treated as such. Does it border on arrogance? Maybe. But we don't deserve to be treated like crap when we are giving our heart and attention out to someone else. Treating someone respectfully should be reciprocated and we need to move on if our needs aren't met. We shouldn't be so afraid to be alone, wasting our time and efforts on someone who doesn't give a damn. Stop defining our self-worth by whether or not we are in a relationship.

Why are some women drawn to jerks again and again? Does he have mystical, animal attraction? Or does she have self-confidence issues? Fix those insecurity issues and the jerks will fall off the map. She'll be able to spot the jerks from miles away and avoid them. But until then, even if she gets rid of the first jerk, another one will come along and she'll repeat the same pattern.

The women don't see their low self-esteem as evidence of the jerk they are with. Even if the woman is smart and stunning, she still needs to believe in herself. She needs to have self-confidence that she deserves to be treated fabulously. Everyone is entitled to that.

Why would you ever choose to be with someone who is not excited to be with you? Where is your self-respect? Stop wasting your precious time on someone who doesn't care enough about you. Delete his number from your phone and move on.

But sometimes logic doesn't always win out. Consider this: you keep ordering a dish you love that contains olives. You hate olives but can't resist getting the mouth-watering dish. You order it anyway and complain the whole way through dinner while you pick out the olives. Rationality dictates to either start liking a dish without olives or tell the chef you don't want them. Either work to change your relationship or leave it.

Lesson #35: You are an amazing person and deserve to be treated like that.

Chapter 36

Scratching my head

I decided to give The Happy-Fun Guy another chance. Two months had passed, but when The Happy-Fun Guy walked up to me on our fourth date, he greeted me with a short kiss when we met for lunch. I told him he could kiss me more than that, but he refused claiming coffee breath. I didn't care; make a move already! I don't encourage sex by the third date, but I hoped to be passed first base by our fourth date. A little tongue would be nice.

During lunch, I asked The Happy-Fun Guy if he was interested in seeing a band with me that Friday night. He wanted to but needed to check his son's schedule first. Fair enough. At the end of lunch, The Happy-Fun Guy quickly kissed me again before he left. An hour later, I texted The Happy-Fun Guy saying, "don't be afraid to kiss me the next time." He replied, "I'll see what I can do... ;)." I was confident that he picked up on my telling him to kiss me more.

Without barking at him like a drill sergeant or critiquing him, I playfully gave him something to think about.

A few days later, The Happy-Fun Guy told me he couldn't go out to hear the band because his son had a basketball game that night. But he asked if I wanted to stop by afterward. I agreed but told him it would be after 11 p.m.

At the same time, I assumed that he didn't think it was a booty call. Even though I was going to his place, I realized I could easily leave if things got too hairy. But, honestly, I didn't envision that happening. Especially since he'd been so reluctant to kiss me before.

When I got to The Happy-Fun Guy's house, he again greeted me with a short kiss. We went inside, sat on his couch, and talked a little. When he kissed me a few more times, the awkwardness flourished. Sometimes someone wants to be tender, but his kiss felt more like, "Ack, I am afraid I am getting cooties!" He slipped his arm around my waist and that was the extent of his move. I wanted to bang my head against the wall in frustration. How hard was this? If a guy likes a girl, he needs to make a move. I said good night soon after that and left his house.

The next morning, The Happy-Fun Guy texted me asking me if I wanted to go to the local indoor farmers market with him for our sixth date. He had never been to my house before, so I sent him my address.

Two hours later, The Happy-Fun Guy sent me a text that said "Here." Seriously? He wasn't coming to my door to get me? Were we in high school and he's the guy who revs his Trans Am in front of my parents' house? If my teenage son ever did that to a girl, I would kick his butt.

While we were at the farmer's market, we ran into a few people that The Happy-Fun Guy knew and chatted with them. When we left the farmer's market, we walked out into the snow and slush. The Happy-Fun Guy didn't even attempt to open my car door. Was he kidding me? Did he not read my online profile that said that I like to go out with men who would open the car door for me? I was freezing, so I didn't stand at the curb and wait for him to come around and open my door.

This man didn't have a clue. Ironically, The Happy-Fun Guy had five sisters. Didn't they teach him how to treat a woman? Maybe they don't understand how to be treated?

Next...

Admittedly, I ghosted The Happy-Fun Guy and didn't contact him again. (Nor did he reach out to me.) I preach not to do that and I utterly failed. I could give the excuse that I took the easy way out, but I should have womanned up and told him that I didn't want to go out with him again.

Lesson #36: It's not your job to teach someone dating etiquette.

Chapter 37

Addendum to The List in Chapter 2

After being out with several more guys, I have a few more things to add to The List.

Continued...

1. Make time for me.

I don't expect or want to see someone every single day in the early stages of a relationship, but I'd still like to see him once a week. Even lunch is fine with me. I think that's a happy medium. And send me a text once a day, simply to say, "How is your day?" That's always a nice gesture.

2. Get me a Christmas gift, a Valentine's Day gift, and a birthday gift.

If I have been seeing a guy since at least October and I get him a gift on December 21st, he'd better make a beeline to the last-minute Christmas sales. I don't expect red roses on our first Valentine's Day, but a small box of chocolates would be nice. And if he forgets my birthday, he'd better start packing up his stuff.

3. If I look nice, throw me a compliment.
If I took the time and effort to look nice for a guy, it would be nice to hear him say that I look good. Everyone likes that.

4. Open the car door for me.
I appreciate when a man has learned how to treat a woman like a lady. He cares about someone besides himself and knows to treat me with respect. Don't ever pull up to my house and send me a text from the car that says "Here."

5. Kiss me.
What can I say? I like affection.

6. If the man has kids, have the same kid-free weekends as me. Conflicting schedules are no one's fault or anything that can be easily changed, but having the same kid-free weekends would be a lot simpler to make plans to see each other. If we like each other enough, we can make it work.

7. If a man likes me, he needs to tell me.
I am assuming that a man does not dig me if he doesn't say anything. He needs to tell me that he likes me. Otherwise, I will assume that I can date other people. Besides, I can't read his mind.

8. The man should be at least a little intelligent.
Smart is sexy to me. I don't expect him to rattle off the chemical formula for sodium chloride, but he needs to know what hair mousse is and that Texas is not the largest state.

Lesson #37: If a man wants a woman of my caliber, he has to work for it.

Chapter 38

Taking Tinder for a spin

Tinder has been around for several years, but I never had the interest to check it out. Until now. Tinder links directly from your Facebook profile, so I easily uploaded a few photos and wrote a short bio about myself. Since it's an app and phone real estate space is limited, I kept my bio short and entered an abbreviated version of my "I believe" speech.

To my surprise, Tinder seemed to be a better concept than a regular online dating site. For those that haven't heard the jokes on late-night TV, Tinder provides a photo and a short bio of someone else on the app. If you aren't interested in them (meaning you don't find them attractive), you swipe left for Nope. If you are interested in them, you swipe right for Like.

The only way two people can match up and talk to each other is if both parties swipe Like. Granted, it sounds shallow, but if I'm not attracted to someone, then I'm simply not. I can't force an attraction to someone nor would I want to. Let's be honest... guys invented the concept.

For the first time, I could choose someone solely based on his looks. Not only was it encouraged, but it was also expected! I wanted to find myself some serious arm candy, with the brain and personality to match.

I liked some things about Tinder. For one, it kept the pool of men under control. Instead of being inundated with many men who randomly contacted me on other sites, the only ones who could message me on Tinder were the ones I chose. I found it more manageable talking to the handful of men that I selected, instead of being contacted by dozens of men who I might not otherwise be interested in. I decided who I wanted to talk to.

Because of the mutual interest, the chance of someone disappearing diminished compared to other dating sites. Nobody likes that. If I decided later that I didn't want to talk to someone, I could always unmatch them.

I also liked the fact that Tinder required everyone to only use their first names. I could view everyone's first name and didn't have to worry about any cryptic usernames to remember who was who. But I had to supply mine as well. Fair trade.

The only thing I didn't like about Tinder was the ability to undo a swipe. My fingers got a little swipe-happy one day and I accidentally swiped left for Nope, completely ruling out a couple of men who I may have been interested in. I couldn't go back and undo it, so they were gone for good. I take that back... if I wanted to pay $20 a month for the premium app, then I could go back. No thanks.

Since matches relied on me swiping Like, it took a little time for someone to contact me. Even if I hesitated thinking I might be interested in someone, he got a left swipe for Nope. I wanted to be sure about someone before giving them a Like. Within an hour, I got my first message.

By being selective, I only talked to a handful of men at one time. Some disappeared, but, honestly, I didn't care. I had lots of options.

I talked to an Army Sergeant who led the Junior ROTC squad at a local high school for about a month. He sent me several paragraphs at a time and seemed interesting. He even told me he felt joy when he got a message from me. However, he never asked me out and eventually disappeared. Even though he initially seemed like a quality guy, I didn't chase him. His unexpected departure mystified me because he found me attractive enough to talk to me in the first place. Even though he told me he was divorced, I wonder if he was married after all and simply wanted some extra-curricular attention?

A softball player contacted me through Tinder. He sent me messages practically daily, but something seemed off with him. My suspicions were already on high alert because he only had one photo on the app and didn't write a bio at all. He flirted with me, but didn't tell me anything about himself and never made an attempt to ask me out. I called him out on it, asking him if he was catfishing me or (yikes!) married. He turned it around without ever answering my questions. Was he bored? Did he need an ego boost? I couldn't put my finger on it. Tired of two months of games, I stopped talking to him.

I met one Tinder guy for a date. He seemed nice, but he did not look like his photo at all. What was he trying to hide? Did he use a five-year-old photo? On our date, he asked me canned questions, like what movies and books I liked. When he asked me out again a few days later, I told him I didn't think that I was the one for him.

Some days, I swiped left for Nope so many times that I maximized my selections for the day. I wondered if I was being too selective. But I wasn't deterred.

Lesson #38: Try different avenues of online dating.

Chapter 39

Not a "chirp-chirp" girl

I went out on a date with someone I had known for many years and had previously gone out with a few times. Even though we didn't have any of those first date jitters and our comfort level pre-existed, I still had high expectations for him.

He came to my door when he arrived for our dinner date, so the night started on a good note. But as we walked off my front porch toward his car, he started walking toward the driver's side of his car. I stood at the sidewalk for a moment and said, "Hey... Hey... Hey..."

He stopped in his tracks and looked at me oddly as if I pointed out a ding on his car that he hadn't noticed.

I then said, "Are you opening my car door for me?"

He turned on his heels, walked toward me, and said, "I thought this had gone away?"

I replied, "No, it hasn't." Was he being a jerk about it and that comment was a precursor for the rest of the night? Or did he honestly assume women didn't want the car door opened for them anymore?

Dinner went well. We sat and chatted for two hours and caught up since we hadn't seen each other in a good six months. After supper, we walked out to the parking lot and he obediently walked over to the passenger side of his car and opened the door for me. He remembered what he needed to do.

See... it works.

Lesson #39: Lessons can be learned.

Chapter 40

My spidey-sense was on alert

One day at work, a friend's husband came up to me and started playing with my hair. Odd behavior, but I didn't say anything and brushed it off. But I made a mental note of it, asking myself, "Who plays with their wife's friend's hair?"

A month later, he did it again. My flirting barometer quickly rose. Was I being overly sensitive or was it all in my head? I decided to talk to Denise about what The Husband did. Friends with the husband, she tried to convince me he was a natural flirt. She said that I imagined everything and, if it bothered me, then I should say something to The Husband. But in the back of my mind, something was up. I couldn't shake it.

A few weeks later, The Husband played with my hair for a third time. Enough is enough. He needed to stop. I didn't want to be a jerk about it, because it was hair, but I didn't like it. I cornered him and told him that he couldn't play with my hair anymore. Someone could witness him and tell his wife. I didn't want to generate any rumors, so I hoped that I squashed it. He laughed it off, feigned innocence, and insisted that his wife wouldn't care. If I found out that my husband played with another woman's hair, I would care.

A couple of months later, I bought a new dishwasher and The Husband volunteered to install it for me. I would save the $80 installation fee. Sure, why not. I agreed only on the condition that his wife was fine with him coming to my house without her and confirmed with her. The Husband and I had always been on friendly terms, but this was the first time that he and I were alone. When he installed the dishwasher, he didn't flirt with me, but I was still a little on edge and didn't want to allow him to do so. I literally and figuratively kept my distance from him.

A few weeks later, The Husband told me that I was evil. What? What did I do? He then proceeded to tell me that he had a sensual dream about me the previous night and it completely threw him for a loop. He said that we didn't have sex in the dream, but that I flirted with him and walked around without much clothing on. I couldn't fault the guy for having a dream about me, because I was guilty of having sexual dreams about other people. However, he didn't have to tell me about it. Did he not realize he risked being on the unemployment line?

A couple of weeks later, The Husband came up to me and told me I was evil again. I asked him if he had another dream. He said no, but confessed that I wandered his thoughts the night before. He then described how he and his wife had sex and he fantasized about me the entire time. Whoa. He wanted my attention and took as much rope as I gave him. I told him I didn't need to hear about their sex life.

I did nothing to encourage this kind of talk from him. I did not flirt with him. I did not tell him anything about my sex life. I was not attracted to him at all and did not want to lead him on. This time the lines didn't blur.

The trifecta came a couple of weeks later. The Husband sent me a text that said, "You're such a tease." What?!? I hadn't done anything out of line and told him I had no idea what he meant. He cornered me and explained what he wrote. An hour earlier, he watched me bend over, playing with my pant leg. He insisted that I purposely had shown him my butt. I laughed out loud. Yes, I did all those things, but I had no idea he ogled me and did not give him a show. He wasn't convinced that I told the truth but I swore that I was. Then he said, "Look what you did to me," and pointed to his engorged crotch. If he had no qualms about showing me his boner, then what was next? I didn't want to find out. I quickly said, "I'm outta here," and walked away.

The Husband was completely out of line and made me uncomfortable being around him. He took advantage of our friendship and it angered me. I hate to admit that my under-reactions escalated his horrendous behavior. I did not do him or myself any favors. But since he was my friend's husband, I wavered between telling her and ruining our friendship, or confronting him and telling him to stop. I chose the latter. However, I struggled with telling him off because we had been great friends for a long time and he crossed a line.

The following week, The Husband ogled me up and down and said, "Very nice." I told him flatly that he needed to knock it off. He replied in a sing-song voice, "I don't know what you are talking about." I said, "Yes, you do know what I am talking about. You are a married man and you need to behave."

An hour later, The Husband sent me a text that said, "If you want me to behave, then I will. But where is the fun in that?" I simply responded, "Yes, I want you to behave." He replied, "Consider it done." I had his word, but I told myself that I'd wait to find out if his actions matched his words. In hindsight, I should have reported him to HR.

The Husband's word lasted two months. I took a new job so I wouldn't be seeing him as much anymore. Upon learning this, The Husband sent me a text that said, "I hope my awesome dreams continue. We'll have to see, now that I don't get to see those legs as much anymore." Ugh.

Lesson #40: Even if a married man is relentless, stay away. Always.

Chapter 41

Ruthless

One Saturday afternoon, I swiped through Tinder, checking out men on the site. I came across an attractive man and stopped for a moment. Up until then, I had been bored with the selection and didn't want to waste my time on someone that I didn't find eye-catching. (And what's up with the men who post no photo at all? Photos are the whole point of Tinder.) When I first viewed this man's profile, in that rare moment, I swiped Like. Immediately the app told me I had a match, meaning at some earlier time, he'd Liked me. Cool.

I sent him a message, asking him how his Saturday afternoon was going. He responded to me within 10 minutes, saying he was watching a movie. I asked him what movie. (Please tell me something smart like *The Shawshank Redemption* or *Gladiator*.) I laughed out loud when he told me *The Shawshank Redemption*. He then asked me if I had plans that night and I said no. He intended to get something to eat at a local restaurant later and asked if I wanted to join him. Hmmm.... that was quick, but I liked his assertiveness. This guy didn't fool around.

We agreed to meet at 6:30 that night. He told me he had a few errands to run first, so I asked him to send me a message if he would be late. He complied.

I arrived at the restaurant a couple of minutes after 6:30, a little embarrassed and ready to apologize for my tardiness. I showed the hostess a photo of the guy and she gasped a little at how attractive he was, then said she hadn't seen him. I sat at the corner of the bar and sent him a message of my location so that he could easily find me. Hungry, I decided to get myself something to eat while I waited for him.

By 7:00, I still hadn't heard from him and sent him a message, asking if he was on his way. Still nothing. I finished eating by 7:15 and checked if he had sent me a message. Tinder showed he had logged on 10 minutes earlier (so he had seen my "Are you coming?" message) and that he was two miles away. I hoped he was on his way, so I decided to give him 15 more minutes.

By 7:30, he still hadn't come and my patience ran out. He couldn't even give me the decency to tell me that he was running late. That's rude, especially on a first date. When I sat in my car, I sent him a final message that said, "It's common courtesy to tell someone when you are delayed or if you won't be showing up at all."

I hesitated before I clicked Send. I wanted to call him out on his bad behavior and that I would not stand for it. I added one more sentence before I hit Send: "Don't contact me again." I dropped my proverbial mic.

Owing this guy nothing, I didn't care that I called him out on his poor behavior. I would never run into him to have to worry about being nice to him. I didn't curse at him or call him names, but I made it clear that I didn't like that he stood me up.

Good thing I hadn't shaved my legs.

Lesson #41: Call someone out on their bad behavior.

Chapter 42

Insecurity rears its ugly head

I like to think I am a confident woman. I have no problem telling off a man who stands me up or going head-to-head with someone who hurts my friend. I'm not afraid to eat dinner by myself or go to a movie solo. But every so often, insecurity gets the best of me. I put my pants on one leg at a time, just like everyone else.

My friend Kevin wanted to host a cookout at his house one Saturday night. He invited me and asked me if it was okay to invite The Accountant and his girlfriend. I wouldn't stir up any drama, so of course, I said yes. Plus, I told Kevin that he needed to tell The Accountant that I was invited too, so he and his girlfriend wouldn't be taken by surprise. I flew solo, but I figured I could mingle with other people I knew. No harm, no foul.

I arrived at the party around 7:00. Kevin immediately told me that The Accountant and his girlfriend were not coming to the party after all. They had other plans. Whew. An awkward moment averted because I hadn't encountered them together yet. Ten of us at the party chatted, told funny stories, and ate some good food. (I brought my famous double chocolate sea salt cookies. Yum!)

Around 10:00, I decided to head home within the hour. Some folks stood outside at the fire pit and a bunch of us sat inside chatting. Several people inside asked me to go out to the fire pit with them, but I declined. They could go outside after I left.

Ten minutes later, I sat on the couch next to Kevin. His phone buzzed with a new text from one of the partygoers out back and he quickly showed it to me. The message said: The Accountant and his girlfriend are here. Come outside.

I won't lie, I panicked a little. I said to Kevin, "Nope, can't do it. Gotta go."

I wasn't ready to spot them together. I would have been fine if The Accountant came alone or if I had a date with me, but I didn't want to be around their coupleness. (Is that even a word?) I'm sure The Accountant would have been cordial to me, but I didn't want to find out. I didn't have any feelings for The Accountant anymore, but I couldn't be around them. I quickly said my goodbyes to everyone inside and headed out the front door.

Kudos to anyone who encounters an ex and the ex's new significant other and can handle that situation with dignity and grace. If you can do that, you're more courageous than I am.

Lesson #42: Insecurity happens to anyone.

Chapter 43

The Nurse

I met The Nurse on Tinder and he was some serious arm candy! He and I sent messages back and forth for a good week and he seemed genuine. He was a couple of years younger than me, never married, and had no kids.

I was tickled that he found time to text me during his shifts. Since he worked odd hours at the local hospital, he didn't have regular weekends off like I did. When he told me he was off for four days in a row, I asked him if he wanted to get together on one of those free days for coffee or a drink. To my delight, he said, "Definitely!"

I hadn't been this excited for a first date in a long time. With almost all of the other people I had met, I had gone in with an indifferent attitude, not expecting much at all. Some of them piqued my interest after a few dates, but none got me excited like this before we met. I had a ridiculous fear that The Nurse wouldn't match his Tinder persona.

On the night of our first date, I arrived at the restaurant 20 minutes early and chatted with the bartender while I waited. When The Nurse walked up to me, relieved that he looked exactly like his photo, he immediately said, "I feel like I have to do this." He leaned in, gave me a giant hug and a kiss on the cheek.

We chatted and shared fish tacos over the next three hours, confirming that it was one of the better first dates I've ever had. We talked continually and the conversation never seemed forced with questions of what movies or books I liked. He did, however, ask me what my favorite color was. I found it odd since we weren't in elementary school picking crayons, but I said purple.

The Nurse was genuine and respectful. He seemed organized and he had no idea how cute he was. We finally decided to call it a night when The Nurse and I were the only ones left in the pub, and the bartender seemed anxious for us to leave.

The Nurse walked me out to my car (where I showed him my purple rain jacket) and we chatted for another 20 minutes. He hugged me and kissed me on the cheek again. He then asked when we could go out again. When I told him I had my kids the following week and my time was limited, his smile faded. I then said, "but that doesn't mean we can't have lunch," and his smile quickly returned. He hugged me again and wished me good night. I also told him my rule about discovering a man's last name.

Five days later, we met for lunch. Again, our conversation flowed. The Nurse was an easy person to be with. He wasn't judgmental and he completely accepted me for who I was. Even the fact that I told him I couldn't wait to watch the upcoming Star Wars movie didn't scare him away. (I'm such a geek sometimes.)

At the end of our lunch date, The Nurse surprised me when he asked, "Is it too soon for me to meet your kids?" Taken aback, I laughed out loud. No one had ever asked me this quickly about meeting my kids. I told him yes, it was too soon (after all, it was only our second date), and I appreciated him asking about it.

Over the next five days, The Nurse sent me lots of cute texts starting with "Hey, beautiful" or "Good morning, sunshine." He turned up the cute factor. But I kept my emotions at arm's length until things got serious. I purposely kept myself from falling for his charm. For all I knew, The Nurse called everyone by cute pet names, so he wouldn't have to remember anyone's name.

On our third date, The Nurse came over to my house for the first time and brought me flowers. Purple. He remembered my favorite color.

A few days later, I told my friend Amy what The Nurse did and she said, "So far, he is doing everything right. If this goes sour," and she pointed at me, "I'm blaming you." Thanks, Amy, I love you too.

I liked what I learned about The Nurse but still didn't want to rush into anything emotionally with him. I didn't want to assume anything until he and I had a conversation about being exclusive. I had been burned too many times in the past for thinking that too quickly.

The Nurse remembered my upcoming birthday, so he asked me 10 days beforehand if he could take me for a celebratory dinner. I was floored. After the crappy Christmas and Valentine's Day I had (ahem... The Great Dane Guy...), I was excited to hear that someone planned ahead for me. We found this little Italian place that didn't seat more than 25 people.

After dinner, The Nurse said to me, "I have to ask you a question."

"Sure, what is it?" I asked. The length of our relationship was way too early for him to be proposing (ha!), so who knew what his question was. Did he want me to go with him somewhere? Did he want me to help him take his car to the shop to get it fixed, so he had a ride home?

The Nurse took my hand in his and said, "Will you... be my.... Girlfriend?" I immediately smiled and said, "Yes, of course." We had only known each other for two weeks. Were we rushing in? Maybe. No red flags emerged with him and I wanted to spend more time with him. Besides, how could I say no to such a sweet proposal? The immediacy held me back, but I told him yes, I would be honored. The Nurse told me that he really, really liked me. We agreed that we would be exclusive and assumed no flirting with anyone else.

Over the next few days, we met up for five days straight and I was happy about everything. I wasn't suffocated at all, even though I liked my independence. On the fifth day, The Nurse inquired about my daughter's upcoming soccer game schedule and asked if he could come watch her play. I think my eyes popped out of my head. I had never had someone make this much effort to meet my kids. I told him I would ask her if she agreed and would let him know. I didn't want to show up to my daughter's soccer game with a random man standing next to me. To my delight, my daughter approved of The Nurse coming to watch her play. (He used to play and coach soccer.) I was a little nervous about their meeting, but she easily accepted him. A few days later, The Nurse met my son when we all made s'mores at my house.

I told The Nurse I had deactivated my Tinder account because the novelty had worn off. I didn't say anything about assuming a future with him. The next day he told me he had done the same. This made me happy because this eliminated any angst-ridden assumptions or fears regarding Tinder activity.

Over the next two months, The Nurse voluntarily fixed my gutter, helped me get some things at Home Depot, easily met my friends, introduced me to his mom, and met my parents when they were in town. Before the end of the second month, he told me he loved me. I didn't experience any awkward moments with him. I was comfortable around The Nurse and Allan approved of him. We spent entire weekends together doing normal, daily stuff like pruning bushes and running to Target. He also changed jobs, so he had weekends off and no longer worked 12-hour days.

One Saturday, we went on a town scavenger hunt with his friends. When our team was six blocks from the meeting point, the clouds above us opened up and drenched us. The Nurse brushed it off. He was a good sport when our team lost and not uber-competitive.

The Nurse and I went to New Orleans with my parents for my mom's family reunion. They say you learn a lot about a person when you travel with them. He and I talked the entire two-hour flight. Neither of us ever had to pull out anything to read. He didn't bat an eye when my mom had a public meltdown and he shrugged off our limited alone time.

The Nurse took it upon himself to fix various things around my house: my front porch, my gate, and my garage door. I've always been one to take care of my home, so it blew my mind that The Nurse wanted to do these things for me. Sometimes I struggled to let him because I'm fiercely independent. But he wanted to take care of me. I'd never had someone want to be there for me like that.

Lesson #43: Patience pays to meet a nice guy.

Chapter 44

Pimpin' ain't easy...

One Friday night, I stopped at the grocery store to get a few things. When I walked down the freezer aisle, a man and his young son lingered in front of the rows of ice cream. I grabbed a carton of mint chocolate chip for my daughter and the father took a step toward me.

"Excuse me," he said to me, "what kind of ice cream do you recommend?"

Everyone's taste in ice cream differs, so how could I possibly recommend a good flavor? Had he never eaten ice cream before? If he asked me about my favorite restaurant, I could have given him some good recommendations.

"Well, what do you like?" I asked.

Then I turned to the man's young son and asked him what he liked. The little boy must have been around eight or nine. He could barely get two words out, as I had put him on the spot. I gave him a few prompting questions.

"Do you like chocolate chip? Or marshmallow? Or Oreo cookies?" I inquired.

The man interrupted me and said, "Well, what is your favorite?"

I chuckled a little bit because my favorite might not be his favorite. I said, "This one," and pointed to the cartons of salted caramel on the bottom shelf.

The man explained that he and his son intended to watch scary movies and eat ice cream. He told me way more than what I wanted to hear, but I played along and listened. I didn't make eye contact with the man and talked primarily to his young son. I hoped he didn't see me roll my eyes.

Finally, the man said, "Well, we'd like to tell you how the ice cream and movie go. Can I get a hold of you somehow?" This man wasted the $5.99 he spent on a book detailing the best ways to pick up women.

The man unabashedly pimped out his young son so that he could talk to me and ask me out. A weird combination of flattery and creepiness swept over me. This was the first time that I was approached in a grocery store like this.

The man had some serious cojones, that's for sure. But his approach was all wrong. Did he always use his kid to break the ice when trying to pick up women? Couldn't he use a line like, "Do these apples smell fresh to you?" without involving his son? Worse yet, did the boy understand what his dad did? Did the boy play along?

I chuckled a little again and said, "That's okay." After all, I was dating The Nurse.

He said, "Okay, no problem."

And I walked away.

Lesson #44: Don't use your kid as a prop to meet prospective dates.

Chapter 45

Passing by

One morning, as I drove my son to work, we passed The Great Dane Guy walking his dog. I hadn't seen him in several months and I blushed as I caught myself staring a little too long as I drove by. I raised my hand a few inches as if to wave, but decided not to. The Great Dane Guy glanced in my direction, but I don't think he recognized my car.

A flush of emotion came over me. I missed him, but I had mixed emotions remembering he was the same person who didn't get me a Christmas gift or a Valentine's Day gift. But yet, he was the same guy who volunteered to drive me home from the hospital. I was determined to find out if I imagined everything that I felt, or if he truly didn't give a shit about me.

A few weeks later, an opportunity presented itself. Kelly and I had plans to hear her boyfriend's band play at a restaurant that The Great Dane Guy had frequented. I texted The Great Dane Guy, asking him about the venue. I hadn't had any contact with The Great Dane Guy in months and I nervously assumed that he would blow off my text. To my surprise, he responded within a couple of hours and sounded happy to hear from me. He didn't write a few monosyllabic words but instead wrote a few sentences.

The Great Dane Guy and I texted several times over the next few days. His messages didn't come all day, every day, but we had a genuine conversation. He sent me a photo of another Great Dane he had adopted and said he was cramped in his bed with both of them. He casually flirted with me, but I kept him at arm's length by taking hours to respond to his texts. I wanted to keep him wanting more.

After a few days, I didn't have anything new to say to The Great Dane Guy without going into a serious discussion about why he hurt me. I didn't start a new topic of conversation and let The Great Dane Guy go. I deleted the text string and his contact info from my phone. I figured if he wanted to date me again, he would have said so, but he didn't. I wasn't begging him. He knew where to find me.

Besides, if The Great Dane Guy and I ever got serious again, I would not share a bed with two Great Danes!

Lesson #45: It stinks when you think you have a good relationship with someone in the beginning, only to have them disappoint you.

Chapter 46

Life partners

After three months of dating exclusively, The Nurse took my hands in his and said to me, "I love you and I see a future with you. I want us to be life partners."

Come again? Did that mean he simply wanted to play house indefinitely or that he wanted to marry me? I wasn't about to guess. "What do you mean by life partners?" I asked expectantly.

He said, "You know, we'd eventually get married."

Wow. We had known each other for mere months and The Nurse decided he wanted to spend the rest of his life with me. I had never met anyone like that before. No one had ever been so immediate with their feelings and what they wanted with me.

I smiled and said, "Okay, I wanted to know." I didn't want him to think I rushed into things, but I was open to the possibility. I needed a little more time to make sure.

Everything was going great with The Nurse, but I felt in my gut something was off with him. Even my daughter picked up on it.

Lesson #46: A guy can meet all of your needs but something can still feel *off* with him.

Chapter 47

Current totals

In the past seven years, I have been on almost 30 first dates. That's a lot! But think about it... 30 first dates over seven years is an average of four a year. Just four. That's one new date every three months. But let's keep in mind that I dated The Professor for three and a half years, so that cuts my timeframe in half. With that, the average is then 10 dates a year. Less than one a month. Those numbers are still somewhat modest. The numbers are even smaller when I count how many second dates I've had, how many men I have kissed, and the even fewer amount that I have slept with.

I had men stand me up, avoid kissing me, tell me they love me after two months of dating, and disappear on me. I had run the gamut on finding someone for me. Good men exist but I wanted to find one that I was passionate about; one that stoked my energy.

How many men did I need to meet before I found The One?

Lesson #47: Date as many people as you want until you find The One.

Chapter 48

I needed to know

A few weeks after I deleted The Great Dane Guy's number out of my phone, he texted me and asked me how I was doing. The good news was he still thought of me in his busy life (coaching two sports, raising three teenage sons, a promotion at work), but the bad news was he took weeks to contact me. Admittedly, I still liked the guy, but I couldn't deal with the yo-yo attention. He was great, but I didn't like the spurts. Maybe he only reached out to me when he had some downtime?

The Great Dane Guy texted me one day, asking if I had any baseball contacts for his regional all-star team. I said I did, but I told him it would cost him a lunch. He chuckled at my hardball but agreed.

We met at a local restaurant on a busy weekday and when The Great Dane Guy walked up to me, he immediately hugged me and leaned in to kiss me. I hadn't told him that I was seeing The Nurse; I turned my face so that he kissed me on the cheek.

Throughout lunch, I found myself blushing and giggling. We caught up and had a good time. At the end, The Great Dane Guy walked me out with his hand on the small of my back, and I let him. He was still manly and sweet. He walked me to my car and leaned in to kiss me again. This time I didn't turn my head and he kissed me on the mouth. I'm sure I blushed. I shouldn't have let him kiss me, but I got lost in the moment.

On a lark a few weeks later, I told The Great Dane Guy I would be driving through his neighborhood because I was dropping my daughter off at a friend's house nearby. I asked him if he would be around and if I could stop by. He said yes and yes. I had something to ask him. But I prepared myself that I might not like the answer he gave me.

When I walked into his house, The Great Dane Guy gave me a huge hug and kissed me on the mouth. I smiled at him but stepped away.

"I need to know something," I told him, "before I... before I... like you again." He gave me an expectant look. Incredibly nervous to ask him, but I wondered many times why he didn't get me a Christmas gift. Did he lose interest in me? Did he find someone else? Was he afraid to take the relationship to the next step? I wanted the answer so that I could move on. Even if it wasn't what I wanted to hear.

"You were fantastic to me when you got me out of the hospital last year and a couple weeks after that," I told him, "but then... but then... When Christmas came around, I got you something and you didn't have anything for me." My eyes swelled, but I held back the tears so that I could continue. "I was extremely hurt because I thought you liked me. I don't understand why you didn't have anything for me." I prepared myself for him to say something terrible like 'because I didn't think about it.' I wanted the truth as awful as it could be.

The Great Dane Guy took a deep breath and finally spoke. "I'm so sorry," he said. "Honestly, I didn't get anyone anything last year, because my dad was so sick and eventually died. Not even my sons."

I breathed a small sigh of relief. This time it wasn't about me. He didn't completely disregard me like the others. The answer wasn't the best, but it wasn't the worst either. The Great Dane Guy spoke again. "I'm so sorry. Do you want to hit me?"

I chuckled and said no. I was happy that I had an answer and that he apologized. This was the third time I didn't get a Christmas present from someone, but the first time that someone truly expressed regret for not doing it.

As much as I liked The Great Dane Guy, he didn't make much effort to talk to me. If I sent him a text, a couple of days passed before he responded. A few weeks later, I permanently deleted him from my phone. I deserved more. I was done wasting my time on someone who didn't adore me.

Lesson #48: If you want to know something and you fear the answer, take a deep breath and ask. Most times it's better to hear the truth than not knowing at all.

Chapter 49

Ten things a guy looks for in a wife

From *Cosmopolitan*... Sounds like a lot of the things that I want in a man:

1. Someone he can trust — not just with going out dancing with the girls, but with all his secrets and weird, dumb fears.
Trust is the foundation upon which all relationships are built, and mutual respect is the mortgage with which you pay for that relationship or something. My point is: Trust is huge for anybody anywhere in any kind of relationship, and it's no different for guys looking for life partners.

2. Someone who supports him even if he suddenly wants to quit his job to pursue his dream of becoming a famous screenwriter/inventor.
Sure, that might sound easy now, but what happens when he loses his job or decides he needs to take a huge chunk of savings and start his own company? Or pursue his dream job at 40? It takes a lot of

patience, love, and understanding to support your partner when times are rough and there's no sign of when it'll get better. And that's a two-way street because guys also want...

3. Someone who has drive and ambition, and doesn't just sit around posting motivational quotes on Facebook.

Personal happiness is key to a healthy relationship. You should have goals as a couple, and also individual goals, and the way you make it work is figuring out how to juggle all of that at once.

4. Someone who wants to spend time with him, but also goes out a few times a month on their own.

I don't think anyone has ever described their perfect mate as "someone who would, if it were possible, literally graft their skin to my skin so we could never be apart." Someone who has their own life and hobbies and passions is always a good thing.

5. Someone he can have really (really, Really, REALLY) great sex with.

Sex isn't the most important thing in the world, but it's up there. To be clear, that doesn't mean every guy is out there looking for their personal sex goddess, just someone they're compatible with; whether that's some vanilla sex once a week or someone they can get kinky with thrice a day.

6. Someone who accepts that maybe he's not the best communicator and understands that he's working on it.

Yeah, people need to get better, but human beings are dumb, weird, stubborn idiots, and we must recognize and accept that in each other. Be forgiving of the little things.

7. Someone who shares his values and ideals, and knows that no matter how much they argue, it will never be about anything serious.

It's important when you get married, but it's even more important when you have kids. Otherwise, they will sense the weak links and destroy you.

8. Someone who keeps surprising him because they're always changing (but not into a werewolf or something, just growing as a person and taking on new challenges).

You know those people who seem interesting at first, and then you realize they have the same three stories that they tell over and over, and that's all they got? Yeah, the opposite of that. But still, not a werewolf.

9. Someone who speaks their mind.

Communication is paramount, so being able to voice what you want, what's going well, and what isn't is incredibly important to a healthy relationship. I guess, alternatively, you could also not care about anything and not contribute to your relationship. That could work too, maybe.

10. Someone who wants to learn about him and grow with him.

You know, someone with whom he can live a long and rewarding life.

Lesson #49: Relationship needs don't discriminate.

Chapter 50

Not The One

After nine months of dating The Nurse, I drove to his house one night to break up with him. I knocked on his door and took a deep breath, deciding that I would break his heart. He seemed excited to see me and motioned for me to come inside. We stood in his kitchen and he told me about his day, as he had every day before.

I took a deep breath and interrupted him, "I don't think we should see each other anymore."

He stared at me blankly as if he didn't understand me.

My heart raced as I tried to form kind words in my head; something I didn't always get when others broke up with me. I wanted to be honest but didn't want to give him any indication that there could be another chance for us.

"You're not The One." Tears streamed down my face. I didn't picture myself spending Valentine's Day with him, hitting the year mark with him, or certainly not marrying him, despite the many times he told me he wanted to spend the rest of his life with me. I had to admit to myself, and him, that I wasn't in love with him. "You need to be with someone who wants to be in this relationship as much as you do," I told him. Tears continued down my face. He didn't shed a tear; I cried enough for both of us.

The Nurse didn't say much back to me as I ended our relationship. I wasn't sure if he was shocked or simply had nothing to say. I repeated many times that he deserved better. An hour later, we walked out to my car. I handed him a box full of items he kept at my house and I drove away, with tears still running down my face.

The week leading up to that night stressed me because I felt sick about ending things with The Nurse. He was a decent man; we never fought, he was attentive and he wasn't a jerk like some of the other guys I had met. But I couldn't force something that didn't exist and I couldn't unfairly let him believe we had a future. He was a nice guy and he adored me, but he didn't thrill me.

I think The Nurse was more in love with the idea of a great girlfriend than he was with me as his girlfriend. Most times I had a gut feeling that he didn't 'get' me. We were so polite and pleasing to each other that we didn't find out what made each other tick. We didn't have deep conversations, nor did he ask about my feelings toward certain things. We didn't share a lot of common interests either.

Seven months in, I found out that The Nurse didn't recall basic things about me. He didn't know my middle name (even though I told him at least twice) and he didn't remember my birthday (even though he took me out for it). When I shut my eyes, he couldn't tell me my eye color even though he looked at me all the time. Maybe he wasn't observant or had a poor memory, but I wanted him to be aware of these basic things about me.

Dating isn't charity. I wasn't in love with The Nurse and I had a right to move on – and so did he. I didn't take the coward's way out by sleeping with someone else or treating him badly until he ended things with me. I reminded myself that he will find someone else. He will break someone else's heart and another guy may break my heart. I had nothing to feel bad about because love is messy as f*ck.

Two weeks after I broke up with The Nurse, he unfriended me on Facebook. At first, I found it harsh, but I understood why he did it.

Lesson #50: If you honestly don't see a future with someone, do the right thing and end it.

Chapter 51

Tips for Guys

I decided to dip a toe into the online dating pool again to see who was out there. This time was more of a social experiment than anything else and I had no expectations at all. I went right to Tinder because I liked the fact that I could pick and choose who contacted me without feeling overwhelmed by quantity. A few things I considered while perusing the photos that might help guys find success:

1. Keep your head and face clear.
No sunglasses or hats. I want to look at your eyes and how much or how little hair you have. I don't care if you are bald. Be your true self. And it's hard to see someone's face if half of it is covered with sunglasses.

2. Post at least three different, recent photos of yourself.
I want to make sure you are indeed a real person and not catfishing me. I suppose you could always use different photos of someone else

and still catfish me, but that takes some effort. Nor do I care what you looked like ten years ago before you lost your hair and gained thirty pounds.

3. Post a full body shot of yourself.

If you only post photos of yourself from the neck up, it makes me think you are hiding something. Like a third arm or an extra 200 pounds.

4. Please, no ab shots.

Dude, even if you go to the gym eight days a week, I don't need to see your abs. And if you are super fit, here's a tip: Don't give away all of your aces. That would be like me posting photos of myself in a bikini. Don't try so hard.

5. Don't post photos of your kids.

You may have good intentions, but creeps lurk online singling out kids Photoshopping their images into some bad pictures. Just don't do it.

6. Avoid group photos as your main photo.

My first question is, "Which one are you?" and then I move on.

7. Skip the unnecessary photos.

I don't need to look at individual photos of your cat, your Mustang, your Harley, the Philadelphia Eagles logo, or a first-place trophy from your softball league. That's what your bio is for.

8. Avoid photos with women, unless it's your mom or a celebrity.

My first thought when I see a woman in the photo is, "Is that your wife or girlfriend?"

9. Smile.

When you smile, it gives me the impression that you enjoy life and aren't so miserable.

As for the bio, I have one rule: Be honest about your intent. If you are looking for a relationship, say it. If you are simply looking to hook up, say that instead. Your honesty clears up any confusion.

A couple of men contacted me about a "no strings attached" relationship. One told me upfront that he was married and was prowling for some action on the side. That kind of relationship wasn't for me, but I appreciated his candor. I would hate to get involved with him, only to find out later that he was married.

Keep in mind that you are an adult, so write like one. Avoid abbreviations, write out a few sentences about yourself, and you'll be fine.

Finally, if you like a woman, ask her out within a couple of weeks. If you wait too long, she might get snatched up by someone else and will be gone.

Lesson #51: Men: Follow these tips for successful online dating.

Chapter 52

The Attorney

The Attorney was one of the first men I connected with on Tinder the next time around. He smiled in all three of his photos and one of those was a full-length shot of him at the beach in the winter. His bio blatantly said, "I am not into games. It's a cliché, but I want to meet someone who is a nice, healthy, intelligent person and is looking for the same..." Wow, that was exactly what I wanted!

In one of my first chats with The Attorney, I asked him what he typically did in his kid-free time. He replied with a huge paragraph that wasn't simply "I hang out and have fun," leaving me to scratch my head at a vague answer like other men I had encountered. When he wasn't taking his nine-year-old daughter and six-year-old son on weekend adventures to Inner Harbor or Philadelphia, he went to cheesesteak festivals, watched up-and-coming musicians in ever-changing art pubs, and wrote short stories fusing Darth Vader and Indiana Jones. Since I was the one with a few published books under my belt, I volunteered to edit his manuscripts.

Over the next week, we compared our deathly fear of snakes, a shared love of good food and well-reviewed independent restaurants, and obscure acoustic musicians like Trampled by Turtles and The Vamps.

When I sheepishly confessed that I hadn't been able to watch a horror movie since I saw the original *Poltergeist* at 11, he divulged that Pennywise did it for him. I couldn't get over how many slight things we had in common.

My giddiness hit a snag when we tried to plan our first date. We discovered that we had our kids at times almost exactly opposite of each other. The only day we both had kid-free time was every other Sunday evening. I quickly looked at the calendar to find the next open Sunday.

"We'll have to make reservations," I texted him.

"Why?" he questioned.

"The next free Sunday is Valentine's Day," I wrote.

"Glad there's no pressure!" he quipped. "I hope you don't mind that your Valentine's Day date is terrified of clowns and snakes."

I laughed out loud.

My nerves kicked in at the thought of meeting him, something I hadn't experienced in a long time. More excited nervous than fearful nervous, but definitely nervous. If he was half as smart and witty in person as he was online, then we would have no problem in person. And please, let him be several inches taller than me.

I showed up at the restaurant a few minutes before him and fidgeted with my gloves with a pit in my stomach while I waited. But when he arrived, I quickly realized I had nothing to be nervous about because we immediately hit it off. (And yes, he was over six inches taller than me.) The waitress had to come back twice to take our order because we were too busy gabbing to look at the menu.

"Here, try this," he said, as he forked his bacon lobster risotto and offered me a bite.

I took the fish in my mouth and realized I hadn't been this comfortable with someone in a long time. For two hours, The Attorney and I sat and chatted, shared food, and laughed.

The restaurant was closing up for the night and neither of us wanted to go home. The Attorney later told me that he had looked around the restaurant at other couples and noticed that none of them talked and laughed as much as we did.

We headed across the street to a dive bar that was still open. Impressed that I drank Maker's Mark without any sissy ice cubes, he was the first guy I had been with who drank bourbon. We continued talking and laughing for another two hours. I got the feeling that he genuinely wanted to learn things about me and wasn't asking me canned questions to pass the time. His eye contact was sincere without being too intense. I couldn't remember the last time I hit it off so quickly with someone.

He wore such an obscure radio show t-shirt under his sport coat that I had to ask who it was. I was relieved that he wore Vans, did a lot of charity work with 100 Men Who Care, and drove an older Prius. He was the most unpretentious attorney I had ever met.

At 11:30, we finally headed out of the bar. I couldn't remember a first date ever lasting that long. On most of my first dates, I wanted to leave after 45 minutes because I found the guy dreadfully boring or I had no desire to see the man again.

The Attorney walked me to my car and we lingered. I stepped closer to him, he reached for me, and we kissed. His kiss was sweet and intimate. He asked if we could talk a little more in my car and I said yes. We both got in and immediately started making out. I didn't stop to think that this was out of character for me. (The Veteran was the last person I kissed like this on a first date.) We talked and joked in between kisses, and kept things light.

At 12:30, we finally said goodnight, although reluctantly The Attorney told me he didn't want to leave me. I couldn't wait to see him again. He kept up with me and aroused my intellect. When he flirted with me, I found myself smiling wide many times. I hesitated to rush into things with him, but everything was easy and natural with him. Would he always be like this? I hoped it wasn't all in my head.

On our next date, we went to an artsy Irish pub that, ironically, featured salsa night. Claiming two left feet, The Attorney still wanted to dance with me. However, we never made it to the dance floor because we spent the next three hours sitting in an intimate corner booth sharing food, kissing, and spilling our secrets. We sat so close to each other that other people could witness how into each other we were. Later that night, when he gave me a quick tour of his house, I drooled over his prized collections of Calvin & Hobbes cartoon books. (I'm such a nerd at heart.)

The next time I saw The Attorney, I met his family. His brother and sister-in-law made us dinner and I spent four hours at their house learning the dynamics of their family. They welcomed me like I was meant to be there.

On our fourth date, he came to my place and cooked me dinner. Who comes to someone else's house, brings the food, and cooks them dinner? He grilled us salmon and served side dishes of roasted potatoes and broccolini. We constantly held hands and kissed in between sentences as we talked.

For our fifth date, we ventured to one of the Coolest Small Towns in America where he spent most of his childhood. After we sauntered down the sidewalks hand-in-hand stopping in antique shops and a chocolate café, we went to his place and snuggled on his couch watching movies. He also lent me one of his favorite books, *The Shadow of the Wind*, because he wanted me to take in the same passion that he experienced when he read it.

He was so anxious that his hands twitched and his mouth quivered when he spoke to me. I reassured him that I was a normal person, exactly like him. My cheeks warmed, discovering that I could make his heart flutter and that he wanted to do anything to please me and make me comfortable.

Interspersed between those dates, The Attorney and I texted each other fun YouTube clips and *Wall Street Journal* articles every day. One day, I sent him a link of Jimmy Fallon and Kevin Spacey doing a skit of *House of Cards* through the eyes of kids. Look it up... funny, funny stuff.

Every night, we talked on the phone for at least a half-hour. Those conversations were better than any other previous date that I had in person with someone else. The Attorney's energy was infectious.

Even though our respective custody schedules conflicted, we made it work. I didn't care that I could go two weeks without seeing him. I liked him that much.

One day at lunch, I said to Denise, "We've been friends for over 10 years now and I am going to tell you something that I don't think you've ever heard me say." She looked at me expectantly. I looked her right in the eyes and said, "I am marrying this guy."

I didn't have answers of how or when, but I *knew*. Of course, I couldn't tell The Attorney all this, because I didn't want to jinx the relationship. Denise was so excited and happy for me that she jumped out of her chair. She recognized I had been selective over the past few years and realized I would never settle. Denise had never seen me this genuinely excited to be with someone. The Attorney was different from every other man I had met. My friends divulged that they saw a noticeable difference in me and enjoyed how happy I was.

I had to stay in my house for a few more years until my daughter went to college, but I pictured myself moving the 45 minutes to be with The Attorney. I honestly envisioned a future with him. In the meantime, I hoped that we would eventually get our kids involved and enjoy our time together.

One night on the phone, The Attorney asked me if I had any initial fears going into our first date. I laughed and told him that I only hoped that he was at least four inches taller than me. He chuckled. I suspected before our first date that we would get along famously. A week later, in between kisses, he whispered in my ear, "I'm so glad I was tall."

Hesitant to tell me about his close female friends, The Attorney wasn't sure of my level of jealousy at the time. I quickly interrupted him saying, "As long as you are okay with my male friends." I couldn't wait for him to meet my friends.

When I asked The Attorney to tell me something about himself that not many people knew, he professed to be a "major weeper" when he watched classic romantic comedies like *The Holiday* and *Love, Actually*. When I disclosed that Justin Timberlake was a guilty pleasure of mine, he sheepishly admitted that he had a man-crush on JT. I told him his secret was safe with me. (Oops.)

Our inner geeks came out with each other. We had intense conversations about *Harry Potter* and *Star Wars*. I wasn't a diehard *Lord of the Rings* fan, but The Attorney jumped at the chance to introduce me and gave me a complete background on the story. We were both saddened by the death of Alan Rickman, who once said, "If only life could be a little more tender and art a little more robust." We could all learn a lot from that.

The Attorney remembered things about me that I forgot I told him. At one time, I must have told him at one point that I didn't like mushrooms. Many days and conversations later, The Attorney told me about a particular dish he ate and said, "Oh, you wouldn't like it because it has mushrooms." I was floored that he remembered.

We compared our favorite recipes, too. The Attorney told me that simply talking about a new savory dish he found online was a food orgasm to him. I told him I couldn't wait to make banana beignets with vanilla bourbon caramel sauce. My taste buds went into overdrive thinking about it. Our biggest debate was over who had the best cheesesteak in Philadelphia. He voted for Pat's and I insisted that Tony Luke's was better.

The Attorney was one of the few people who I told about the first guy who broke my heart 25 years earlier. Surprising myself, I felt comfortable telling him things that not many people knew about me. He wanted to understand more about me and told me he talked to his friends about me. I never doubted if he liked me as much as I liked him.

The Attorney was a good dad, too. He understood what it was like to always be on the go with the kids like I was. He took his daughter to tap dancing on Tuesdays and his son to swim meets on Saturdays and volunteered at their events.

He sent me photos of his kids on their way to school, the scenic clouds after a rain, and the tasty pho he ate for lunch. He shared everything with me, even when I couldn't be with him.

The Attorney was the last person I talked to every night before I fell asleep. I hated saying goodnight to him because I wanted to keep talking to him – evident on our marathon first date. He constantly told me how much he loved hearing my voice and wanted me to tell him where I sat in my house so that he could imagine what I looked like talking to him. I was constantly happy every day and, even though I had a lot on my plate, life seemed easy and manageable.

He was a fantastic combination: masculine, gentle, kind, intelligent, cool, fun, and sexy. Everything I've always wanted but never thought I would find. We had an odd kid schedule, but he purposely made time to talk to me and get together. I never questioned whether or not I would see him because we always figured it out. He didn't rush in and tell me he was falling for me without getting to know me inside and out, even though I secretly hoped he did.

Lesson #52: Allow yourself to fall hard and fast.

Chapter 53

Friends with Benefits

As long as men and women exist, an ongoing debate will exist about whether or not men and women can be friends without sexual attraction getting in the way. More men than women believe it won't work which is probably why more women have male friends than vice versa.

I think it depends on the situation. I have lots of male friends who I would never want to have sex with, not because they are unattractive, but because I know WAY too much about them and I could never think about them that way. However, I have never asked if they would want to have sex with me. But so far, those guys who I don't want to be with have never crossed a line, so everything is copacetic.

But what happens when a friend does cross a line? How do the friends keep from making it weird? Or is it even possible to stay friends with someone and get the benefits?

You love this person like a best friend and would do absolutely anything for them, but you are not in love with them. You tell this person to get their head out of their ass and not offend them. Because they love you like a best friend, too, and understand that you only want the best for them and they take your advice.

On some drunken night, when they are pouring their soul out to you (because they know you won't judge them) and they get all sentimental and tell you how amazing you are and that they are thankful to have you in their life, you kiss them on the cheek. And you think about moving your face a couple more inches, toward their mouth.

In your mind, it feels amazingly good. You are close enough with your friend to tell them that you are thinking about this, something you might not always do with someone you just met for fear they might think you are weird. But your friend already knows that you are weird and loves you for it.

Could the kissing lead to so much more? Or is it the alcohol talking? And if it does go further than kissing, what will happen? If you've been friends for 25 years, why can't you still be friends for 25 more? Would sex get in the way? Or would it make things better?

If you both want the closeness of sex, because you are already so close, then I say, "Go for it."* If you want a purely physical relationship and keep everything in perspective, go to someone you know and trust. Why on earth would you go to some stranger you just met?

*ONLY reap the benefits if you are both single.

Lesson #53: It's okay to have sex with your friend – as long as it is just sex.

Chapter 54

Hacking online dating
...or how a self-professed nerd ran an algorithm to find the man of her dreams

A woman named Amy wanted to get married but didn't want to settle (Hmmm...sounds a lot like me...) so she published a TED talk describing what she did. She ran the numbers calculating how long it would take once she met someone to be in an exclusive relationship, get engaged, get married, and eventually have a child. She quickly realized she should have started five years earlier.

Amy had certain criteria she wanted from a man and he had to meet them or she wouldn't even consider going on a date with him. Was she being too picky? Her Jewish grandmother was convinced. Despite her Bubbe's push to let serendipity do its thing, Amy utilized her love of numbers and JavaScript to develop a spreadsheet to track what she wanted in a man.

She created an online dating profile and went out with a lot of different men. She realized that some of them were good men, but not for her. Then she created her questions instead of the canned ones from the dating site. Did anyone care if she was a dog person? Probably not. She wanted to figure out if someone worked hard, but not too hard, and if they would ever travel to an obscure place like the banks of the Jordan River.

Amy then created a database stemming from her 72 questions and ranked them in order of importance to her. Being Jewish was #1 on her list. Being able to challenge her was a close second. Understanding the difference between the works of Monet and Cezanne hit the bottom. Each of the questions was weighted and the possible men had to score a minimum of 700 points before she even agreed to email them, let alone go on a date with them. (Surely, her grandmother spewed Jewish curses at her by this point.)

Almost immediately, Amy found an online profile of a man who met all of her criteria. The only problem was he didn't like her back. She rethought her algorithm. The one factor she had previously ignored was her competition. Amy comprehended that she was a catch and sensed in her mind she was leaps and bounds above the silly, skin-baring women claiming to be "fun-loving" grabbing every shallow man's attention with visual stimulation of simple cleavage.

But Amy wasn't deterred. She came up with a plan to create 10 fake male profiles, which she would use to gather data. (Don't worry, she wasn't catfishing). Amy didn't want everyone's data on the site; only the data on the women who would be attracted to the type of man that she wanted to marry. (Even though this plan was a helluva lot of work, it seemed brilliant to me.)

Amy looked at qualitative data regarding humor, tone, voice, communication style, the average length of a profile (under 100 words), and how much time was spent before responding to messages (usually a day). In reviewing her data, Amy realized she needed to be more approachable, but without dumbing down her profile. She also adjusted her photos to show a little more skin from the matronly look she previously posted.

After a few months, Amy's real profile was the most popular online and many men wanted to meet her. However, she was still selective because few of them met her original point system. (By this time, her whole Jewish family was getting frustrated with her. They wanted another baby in the family.) She finally agreed to meet a man who met her point minimum. They went on a marathon 14- hour date and his points almost doubled by the end of it. Amy eventually fell in love, married the man, and found her Jewish Prince Charming.

What does Amy's story teach us? That it's okay to be picky and not settle. Don't waste your time on someone who gives you blah feelings. Can you wait for serendipity to happen? Not always.

Take matters into your own hands to figure out what you want and what is important to you. Do you want a long-haired beach bum who owns a surf shop and sleeps in until 10 a.m. every day because he works late? If that's your thing, then go for it. Or do you want someone who might not have all of his hair, but gets up at 5 a.m. to make sure he is home by 4 p.m. for the kids' soccer games? Either way, find someone who respects you, treats you like an equal, and makes your toes curl. Don't settle for someone who doesn't.

As for me, things are looking good with The Attorney. (One night, we had a deep discussion about how Barney, not Ted, was the real romantic on How I Met Your Mother.) But if things don't work out, you can be sure I'll be running Amy's algorithm.

Lesson #54: Take matters into your own hands to find the person of your dreams.

Chapter 55

How do you know?

Blogger Paul Hudson wrote this article for any man questioning if he has found the girl of his dreams:

Love is complicated.

How do you know if the woman you're with now is the one you should spend your life loving? Do you "just know" or are there practical questions you should be asking yourself?

Is there some sort of checklist or guide?

Love seems mysterious, and maybe even impossible to define. People often say that words fail to appropriately capture love. I, for one, believe it isn't the words that fail. It's the people who use them.

Love is a natural, logical result of two compatible souls meeting. The real question is: What's "just right"?

You can find the answer through a few simple questions.

1. Has your life drastically improved since you met her? Are you happier? Do you have a better outlook on life? Do your

problems seem less dire and more manageable? Do you have more good days than bad days now? If all of this is true, she may well be "The One."

2. Do you smile every time you see her, think of her, and talk to her?

If you do, then you're in love — and that's the most important sign. If you feel happy being reminded of her existence, then what you have is true love. If the thought of her makes your day a little better — if having her around feels natural and right –then you may have a keeper on your hands.

The woman you should spend your life with is the one you'd rather have by your side than out of reach. She's the woman who's made herself a positive force in your life. If you love her, she well may be The One.

3. Can you talk to her for hours on end without getting bored or feeling awkward?

Sexual passion is important in a romantic relationship. There's no denying that. However, there are more important factors to look for. For example, your partner must stimulate you intellectually — and vice versa.

As you get older and your libido is on the low, you could pop some blue pills (and you most likely will), but sex will no longer be so important. Conversation and companionship are what will hold you together. Love and friendship will make your relationship last.

4. Is she there for you?

The key to finding an amazing life partner is finding someone who lives up to her role in your life. Is she truly your partner, or is she your "girlfriend"? Is she there for you when you need her to be? Is she someone who supports you, motivates you, and keeps you on track?

People in relationships indeed need to maintain their personal identities. But two people in love are there for each other.

5. Has she opened up to you and let you into her life?

It takes some people longer to open up, even with the people they truly care about. Everyone's expression of love is unique. The way you love her might be different from the way she loves you. You need a woman in your life who loves you with every atom in her body. Never settle for less.

Lesson #55: Things will be easy when you meet The One.

Chapter 56

Punched in the Gut

On the morning of my sixth date with The Attorney, he called me.

"I want you to know I won't be coming tonight," he told me.

Disappointed, I said, "That's okay, we can reschedule."

"No," he replied, "I'm not coming at all." He took a deep breath and spoke again. "I don't think we should see each other anymore. I'm so sorry."

What? Where did this come from? Did I miss something? I couldn't breathe like I got the wind knocked out of me and my legs collapsed beneath me. This was the same guy who had told me a week earlier that he only wanted to date me exclusively. A few days earlier, we had planned a day the following month to play hooky from work. This was the same guy who kept in constant contact with me all day, every day for the past six weeks, telling me how much he liked me.

"F*ck," I whispered, the only phrase escaping from my mouth. "F*ck," I said again, at a loss for words, embarrassed that the only thing I could say was an overused expletive.

"We can't see each other anymore because of our conflicting kid schedules," The Attorney explained. "I'm so sorry."

I grasped what he said, but we'd been making it work. I wished he would have talked to me about his concerns, before deciding on his own. We had always made time for each other when we checked our respective calendars to figure out how to get together. We talked on the phone every night, learning more about each other.

"Did something happen recently?" I finally found my voice. "Did I say something to make you come to this conclusion?"

"No," he answered.

I had no reason not to believe him. But I was completely blindsided. I found it so hard to fathom that his feelings took a 180-degree turn in a few days. This made me question if everything had been all in my head. I couldn't believe it.

We had only been talking for six weeks. Yes, I realize it was a short amount of time, but we hit it off right out of the gate. Everything was effortless. I fell hard and fast. And he seemed to reciprocate. I hadn't felt this comfortable this quickly with anyone in over 20 years. Sure, I didn't know everything about him, but I had hoped to find out more. Did he pay his bills on time? Would he take care of me and the house when I was down and out with the flu? Could he fix a leaky faucet? This total change of heart made no sense to me.

"I have something to tell you that you can take however you want," I told him. Being vulnerable and knowing that he might not respond, I wanted him to hear it anyway. "I was starting to fall for you." I exhaled knowing it was a huge thing for me to admit.

"I'm so sorry," he repeated.

What was he not telling me?

I slowly hung up the phone and wondered if someone said to The Attorney, "Yes, you like this woman, but how will you make it work?" Maybe that got in his head and he freaked out. Did he take the easy way out and end things with me, so that he wouldn't or couldn't completely fall in love with me while struggling to figure out the logistics of the relationship and our respective kids?

Several of my friends suggested that I ask The Attorney the real reason that he ended things with me. I only had one question for him: Did he break up with me because he didn't picture a future with me and everything was in my head? If the answer was no, then why did he break up with me? If the answer was yes, then that would have crushed me. But at least it would have been the truth.

My best friends worried about how heartbroken I was and tried so hard to keep me distracted so I wouldn't wallow on my couch. They stopped in to visit me. They took me out for dinner, drinks, a St. Patrick's Day Parade, and an art gallery. Allan and Colin wanted to shake The Attorney by his shoulders and say, "What the f*ck is wrong with you?!"

In a valiant effort to cheer me up, Allan even broke a vow of silence and told me the real reason that The Veteran ghosted me over two years earlier. (He claimed the statute of limitations had passed.)

I can't disclose it here, because I promised Allan I wouldn't say a word, but at least it made sense to me after all this time. As I suspected, The Veteran's vanishing had nothing to do with me. Several of my friends even offered up single men that they knew. I told them I wasn't ready to date anyone new yet but appreciated them thinking about me.

I cried for a week. In my kitchen. On my commute home from work. While I walked my dog. I had no appetite and lost a few pounds as a result.

I couldn't sleep for two weeks. My blues were evident over the phone when a stranger asked me if I was okay. I hadn't experienced this kind of heartbreak in years. Decades.

When I told my friend Nicole the whole story of how I met The Attorney and how I fell hard and fast, her eyes swelled full of tears for me. But her fiancé Chris said, honestly and bluntly, "This guy broke your heart. Don't ever give him the time of day again." Easier said than done sometimes. Several other friends asked me what I would do if The Attorney ever tried to ask me for another chance. Getting dumped by him once was tough enough. I didn't think I could do it a second time.

I think The Attorney made a mistake for walking away from something so awesome. I was so certain I would be with him for the rest of my life. Mystified by what truly happened, I might never learn the real reason for his decision to end our relationship. But I hope he eventually regrets it.

* * * *

Three weeks after The Attorney broke up with me, I drafted the final chapter of this book and I sent the full manuscript to him because he always asked me what I wrote about him. I also returned the book he lent me. I wanted him to read that I believed he made an err in judgment for ending things with me. I didn't expect to hear from him at all, as I hadn't had any contact from him for three weeks. (Nor had I reached out to him.)

A few days after I sent him this manuscript, he sent me a text, at 2:30 a.m. The message said: "Got it today. Just finished it. Every page." He wrote something about scattering the pages because they'd come undone, but that was insignificant to me. Clearly, he was reaching out to me.

I didn't want to seem anxious by immediately replying, so I waited 12 hours before responding. I said something like: "Good thing the pages were numbered and others stayed up reading it too." I ended with: "Now you know everything."

He didn't respond. I found it odd that he texted me in the middle of the night. Did he want me to wonder what he was thinking? Did he have unresolved feelings? I waited two days and called him. He didn't pick up, but I left a message assuming that he wouldn't call back to answer my question as to why he texted me so late. His actions from that night didn't make sense to me. And then I deleted him from my phone.

Three months went by...

The Attorney unfriended me on Facebook. I found it odd since he was the one who ended things with me, and also since so much time had passed. Allan and Colin had a theory about why The

Attorney cut off ties with me. A week before he unfriended me, I posted a vacation photo on Facebook of myself wearing a bikini at a Mexican beach. Both Allan and Colin tried to convince me that The Attorney couldn't handle seeing how good I looked and didn't want to be reminded of me, so he completely cut me off to avoid any temptation to watch what was going on in my life. Possibly The Attorney unfriended me for another reason, but the timing screamed coincidentally.

Maybe I fell for an idealized version of The Attorney? I expected better from him based on the person that I thought he was. When he realized he clearly couldn't maintain that version of himself, he hollowed out and cut bait. Real reasons existed for why he left, even though he may have been too ashamed to share those explanations with me.

He wasn't strong enough for me. Not strong enough to trust me with his thoughts and not strong enough to share the truth about why he didn't want to continue. He created a fire that was doused before it could ever run its course. I wasn't with him long enough to understand the depth of his flaws.

Maybe he was into games after all?

Lesson #56: Even if you feel completely in love, someone can still blindside you.

Chapter 57

Closure

After a year of silence, The Attorney sent me a "Please add me to your LinkedIn network" message. When I first read it on my screen, I was in complete shock. The pit in my stomach made me feel like I would throw up. I kept re-reading the simple stock invitation from the site and dropped a few F-bombs each time.

What was he up to? Was he trying to ease his way back into my life in a safe, discriminating way because he was unsure how I would react? Was he sorry about the way he ended things? Did I still haunt him? Was he having second thoughts? I'd think if someone didn't want to have anything to do with their ex anymore, they wouldn't reach out like this. I didn't with any of my exes: The Professor, The Volleyball Player, The Accountant, The Nurse.

I hate to admit it, but The Attorney brought out feelings in me that I had tried to suppress for a year. I shed some tears over the shock of hearing from him. As subtle as it was, he had come back into my life and I struggled with what to think. I wanted to hurl a fire hydrant at him for the pain he caused me.

Despite that almost all of my friends told me to tell him to F*ck Off, my curiosity and maturity got the best of me. Intentionally making The Attorney sweat a little, I waited a few days before I accepted the LinkedIn request. His bio stated that he had made Partner at his law firm while I was out of touch with him. Good for him.

A few days later, I sent him a message congratulating him on his promotion. I assumed he wouldn't answer because of the yearlong silence. To my shock, he replied later that week and apologized for not getting back to me sooner. (Ironic that he didn't apologize for the lengthy absence in my life.) He sent me a second message, again apologizing for the delay in getting back to me, but refrained from writing anything too substantial. I replied trying to be cool and cordial, but still suspicious of his intentions.

Did he expect his LinkedIn invitation to be a first step or a last step? Maybe, in some small way, he found himself some closure by extending the minuscule olive branch. I didn't hear back from him for a month, nor did I initiate a conversation with him.

Two months later, I had plans to be in his town for a work meeting. I hesitantly emailed him through LinkedIn asking if he wanted to meet me for lunch, assuming that he would either decline or not respond at all. To my surprise, he responded the next day. He admitted he already had lunch plans with his staff but immediately asked if I could stick around town and meet him later in the afternoon. Shocked by his offer, I rearranged my afternoon schedule to meet him at a WiFi café a couple of blocks from his office.

My meeting ended earlier than expected so I headed over to the café. I worked for two hours while I waited for The Attorney. My nerves kicked in a few times since I hadn't seen him in over 18 months. I had so many questions to ask him and part of me wanted to put him on the spot.

I wore an emerald blouse that accented my eyes, a short black skirt, and the same black heeled boots that I wore on our first date. Even though I had moved on and had been dating someone else for a year, I wanted him to see what he gave up.

When The Attorney walked in, he immediately hugged me. We talked for an hour about what had been happening in our lives for the past year. He talked to me with so much attentiveness as if we *hadn't* been out of touch for a year.

I fully intended to ask him hard questions: Why did he abruptly end things with me? Why did he reach out to me after all this time? But, as we talked, the answers didn't matter to me anymore.

As we lingered at the door of the café saying our goodbyes, The Attorney hugged me again. He said, "Keep in touch."

"I will try," I answered, fully knowing that I probably wouldn't. I turned and walked down the sidewalk happy and at peace.

Before I arrived home 45 minutes later, The Attorney texted me: "Good to catch up. Let me know next time you are in town :) Safe driving!" I didn't recognize the random number at first because

I had deleted his contact info from my phone over a year earlier. The first words out of my mouth were "Holy f*ck."

Obviously, he still had me in his phone contacts. Maybe he didn't have closure after all? I waited an hour before cordially responding. I deleted his message from my phone later that night, without saving him into my contacts.

I deserved so much better.

* * * * *

Three months later, this book was published. The Attorney and I had some occasional interaction within that time, so I virtuously sent him a printout of this book so he wouldn't be blindsided and finally told him I was dating someone else. Two weeks later, he responded by blocking me on Facebook and LinkedIn. His immature behavior baffled me because, after all, he was the one who broke up with me two years earlier. That would be like if I blocked The Nurse. His behavior didn't make sense.

Did The Attorney still have feelings for me and was hurt or angry that I moved on? What did he expect to happen?

Lesson #57: Closure doesn't always equal answers.

Chapter 58

Ladies, tear out this chapter and post it on your fridge

You are awesome and deserve to be treated that way. Remind yourself not to put up with the nonsense (these pages are single-sided on purpose).

Follow these tips and you'll be happy:

Stable of Studs

1. If you don't hear an "I like you" by the third date, move on. Plenty of other men are willing to meet you.

2. Make him wait at least two months for sex.

3. If he takes more than a day to get back to you, move on. If he likes you, he will find a way to text you during working hours. Everyone gets a lunch break.

4. You had your own life before him (and your own car and house). Don't let any man shame you for what you have accomplished.

5. Be ruthless and don't make excuses for him. If he doesn't make an effort to be with you, then he doesn't care and never will. If he isn't a naturally kind person, you cannot force him to become one. Always remember: Mean doesn't go away.

6. If possible, meet him for a weekday lunch on a first date. Lunch is usually casual and has a built-in end time to get back to work.

7. If you have been dating for at least six weeks and he doesn't get you a Christmas present, a Valentine's Day gift, or a birthday present, you are an afterthought to him and he doesn't care about you. Dump him.

8. Expect him to open that car door for you and walk you to your door. He also needs to escort you to your car if you drove separately.

9. If he doesn't want to meet your kids or keeps his kids from meeting you, he isn't interested in your whole package. Dump him.

Stable of Studs

10.   Go to the grocery store together as a litmus test to experience how he handles everyday things.

11.   Remember that you are awesome and you deserve someone who treats you with respect and dignity. You deserve attention, affection, and appreciation.

12.   If you are only having sex with him, you are NOT dating him. Have fun if you want, but feel free to date other men. And always be safe!

13.   Don't be the side chick. You are not a consolation prize.

14.   If he stands you up, call him out on it. This is common courtesy, people.

15.   When the relationship ends, delete him from your phone. Take away any temptation to call or text him, or the opportunity to accidentally send him a text that was meant for another man. (Oops.)

16.   Don't ignore red flags.

17.   If he makes you cry sad tears more than twice, dump him.

18.   Always get his last name before agreeing to a second date. Look him up to make sure he doesn't have a criminal record. Hopefully, he is keen enough to do the same thing with you. Most states have a public website to look up anyone's criminal background. Bookmark this site.

19.   Always tell a friend where you are meeting on a first date. Send her a photo of the guy and text her when you leave. Being safe is never a bad thing.

Stable of Studs

20.   Openly date around. Don't narrow it down to one guy until you talk about being exclusive. Assume that he is going out with other women.

21.   Don't chase him. I'll say it again - **Don't chase him**. If he doesn't return your call or text after the second attempt, delete him from your phone. Or, if you are feeling bold, call him out on it. If he gives you his number, you text him and he doesn't respond, tell him you are not into games, and call him out on his bad behavior.

22.   Don't fight for someone who doesn't fight for you.

23.   If you want to get married, don't move in with him unless you have a ring on your finger and a date on the calendar.

24.   If he disappears or unexpectedly breaks up with you, it will hurt and you might never get an explanation, but accept it and move on with your life. He has issues that you are lucky to avoid.

25.   When you do get that awesome guy, be upfront and honest with him. Don't play games and, for goodness sake, leave the drama at home. He deserves a good woman, as much as you deserve a good man.

Lesson #58: Set some guidelines and expectations for yourself and your possible partner before you start dating them.

Chapter 59

The End?

When I met The Attorney, I was so certain that the end of this book would be about me having a fantastic future with him. Turns out, I have no idea what is in store for me. I still believe in love, but it hasn't found me yet. I believed The Attorney was the one for me because he encompassed everything I thought I wanted, but what do I know about love? He hit every one of my benchmarks without even trying, but the whole thing imploded on me. Murphy's Law of Dating reflected our relationship: If something seems too perfect, it probably is.

I'm not sure what the future holds for me. Regardless, I'm starting a clean slate. I have touched on everything here that I wanted to talk about and I don't want to bore my readers. Frankly, I can only talk so much about online dating and having meh feelings for someone. Maybe I need to do something different, like volunteer? I now have an educated perspective based on my trials and I've learned a lot along the way.

Here are some of the significant men I've met on my adventures and the lessons I've learned along the way. Maybe my experience will help you avoid similar dating pitfalls:

• The Professor. Don't ignore red flags. Not the first. Not the second. Not the third. If something seems *off*, it probably is. This relationship lasted well past its expiration date because I wanted so much for it to work after my failed marriage.

• The Veteran. It's okay for you to rush in, but give yourself time between relationships. And if someone disappears, promise yourself that you won't track him down demanding answers. I'm proud of myself that I didn't.

Update: Allan had a 50th birthday party in 2023 and The Veteran and his new wife were there. I hadn't seen The Veteran in almost 10 years since our one and only date. I had moved on and so had he. When his wife stepped away, The Veteran said to me, "Now that my wife is out of earshot, I wanted to tell you that I'm sorry about how things went down with you." Nearly falling off my chair, I told him I appreciated it. He explained what had happened in his life at that time and I got caught in the wake. His sincerity and remorse blew me away. Even ten years later, his apology was heartfelt. He gave me unexpected closure.

• The Usher. Super nice men exist, but if you only have a friendship, don't push for anything more. Let him come to you. If he doesn't, you still have a great friend.

- The Volleyball Player. Even if a guy is hot and gives you the best knock-around fun you've had in a long time, it doesn't mean he is The One. Enjoy it and move on.
- The Accountant. Never shed a tear over a guy who refuses to meet your kids.
- The Great Dane Guy. A man needs to make time for you. You deserve someone who wants to talk to you every day, even if it's a simple text asking how your day is. And if he doesn't get you a Christmas present, he isn't worthy of you.
- The Nurse. Even if he completely adores you (or thinks he does), if your gut tells you that he isn't The One, do the right thing and end it. Let him be in a relationship with someone who wants to be there as much as he does. Dating isn't charity.
- The Attorney. Give your whole heart and don't be afraid to express your feelings. It might not work out. Take the leap anyway.

I believed I would tell you I had a happy ending, but I don't. I hope to find that awesome love someday that makes me feel wonderful, respected, and adored. I deserve a man who loves me so much that the idea of going days or weeks without seeing me would simply be so painful that he would never choose to do it. I want to find love that I will never grow out of, that completely takes me by surprise, kicks me in the ass, and leaves me breathless.

I want a man who tells me during a pool party among a dozen screaming kids that he's in love with me. I want a man who tells me how lucky he is to have me and doesn't ever want to spend time without me. I want a man whose love for me never falters. I want a man who only has eyes for me and tells me that I am beautiful, even after I wake up. I want a man who never lets me forget how much he loves me and adores me. I want a man who will attend a wedding with me and spend most of the night on the dance floor with me. I want a man who intrigues me and inspires me to be a better person.

Until then, I have to take heed to what Thomas Edison said on his path to inventing the lightbulb: "I have not failed. I've found 10,000 ways that won't work."

All it takes is one.

Lesson #59: Have hope.

###

Acknowledgments

Thank you Mom and Dad for the title of this book. When I was a boy-crazy teenager, you both referred to all the boys who I dated as my Stable of Studs. Who knew that I would be writing about it later?

Many thanks to all of my friends who are mentioned here:

Chris, Tom, Carol, Kelly, Lynn, Kristin, Denise, Catharene, Niki, Allan, Cathy, Christi, Michele, Mike, Kevin, Paul, Holly, Nicole, Chris, Amy, and Colin

I love you all.

Stable of Studs

Thank you for reading my book.
If you enjoyed it, won't you please take a moment to leave me a
review at your favorite retailer?
One or two sentences are perfectly fine.
Help an author out. ☺
Thanks!

Want some cool merch from me?
Post a pic of this book on your social media and tag me!
@marywalshwrites

Tag me on:

**Sign up for my sometimes-monthly newsletter and
order autographed books at:**

marywalshwrites.com

Follow me on Goodreads and Amazon:

www.goodreads.com/goodreadscommarywalshwrites
www.amazon.com/author/marywalsh2